Intercession

The Uncomfortable Strategic Middle

P. Douglas Small

An Alive Publication

In association with
Alive Ministries: PROJECT PRAY
Kannapolis, NC

Intercession - The Uncomfortable Strategic Middle

ISBN: 978-0-9986034-1-4

Copyright © 2009 by P. Douglas Small

Published by Alive Publications
a division of
Alive Ministries: PROJECT PRAY
PO Box 1245
Kannapolis, NC 28082
USA

All rights reserved. No part of this publication may be reproduced, stored in a retrieval system, or transmitted in any form by any means (printed, written, photocopied, visual electronic, audio, digital or otherwise) without the prior permission from the publisher. The exception being brief quotations with appropriate reference documentation and the use of the material for teaching and training.

All scripture quotations, unless otherwise indicated, are taken from the New King James Version®. Copyright © 1982 by Thomas Nelson, Inc. Used by permission. All rights reserved.

First Printing 2009
Revision Printing 2011
Third Printing 2018

Cover Photo: Igor Zhuravlov; www.123rf.com
Chapter Artwork: Unico Anello; wikimedia.org
Andrey Kuzmin; www.123rf.com

Dedication

To the nameless, unrecognized saints who pray often,
alone, with passion.
And whose prayers secure an entrance to some closed door,
soften hard hearts, and build bridges to cultures that will hear
the gospel for the first time.
To those who wrestle in the night for the lost, who diligently take
their time on the intercessory wall.
To those whom God places in some uncomfortable middle and
whose persistence in prayer changes not only lives, but nations.

Contents

Section One
Adam, Jesus, the Church and the Middle

1. **Adam: Created for the Middle..................... 11**
   The first Adam was created for the middle. That ground was lost in the fall, and Lucifer seized the high ground enthroning himself as the god of this world. The leader of a band of deceptive rebel thugs, more powerful than man, Lucifer has taken Adam's house hostage. Those born into Adam's family are born slaves. No son of Adam can liberate them. No one can overthrow the Evil and Dark Lord.

2. **Jesus Reclaims the Middle 27**
   Christ came, as a man, as a 'Trojan baby,' to reclaim for mankind, the disputed middle. The battle is not over heaven, but over the earth – over Adam's house! He came to liberate Adam's house. He resisted temptation. He triumphed at the cross. He led captivity captive. He was received into heaven – as a man! Having consolidated "all authority" in his name, he sat down on David's throne and is now our King. Though he reigns in exile, he is ready to return when our mission is complete.

3. **Mankind and the Redemptive Middle 39**
   Now redeemed believers – the Church, the bride partner of Christ, left in the earth as a witness – must hold the strategic, bloody and critical middle by intercession. Satan, defeated, still claims it as his own. Intercession is therefore fraught with warfare. Until all things are under his (Jesus) feet, the middle will continue to be contested. The fallen angelic rebels refuse to acknowledge the cross, the resurrection, the enthronement! They plan a last ditch effort to hold on to the planet! It will fail. It is failing now.

4. **The History of the Recurring Abandonment of the Middle** 53
   Sadly, the people of God have never quite understood their call to the middle. After Adam's tumble, God called Abraham to the center of the ancient world – the land bridge connecting three continents. It was here that Yahweh established His people – in the middle. All were to be priests, a nation of priests. They rejected their role in the middle, choosing to be exclusive rather than graciously inclusive. Isaiah issued the call to the priestly middle for those returning from Babylon. They too, rejected the call to the middle. Jesus, with the scroll of Isaiah in his hand, accepted the challenge. First, twelve were gathered to the middle around him, then 120 in the upper room. Those who turned the world upside down did so from the middle. They could not imagine a church that would retreat to the comfortable end, and abandon the middle. But the Church did just that. Martin Luther, in the Reformation, again rallied believers to the middle – then again the Church chose the end. The cycle seems endless.

5. **The Final Call to the Middle** 77
   In the end, a Church will arise, a faithful bride-partner, and will humbly stand down the Evil One. The middle will not be abandoned. The faithful bride-partner will reach every tongue and tribe in Adam's house with the good news. With garments unspotted and hearts turned to heaven, they will meet the returning Christ in the air.

Section Two
Jesus Teaches on the Middle

6. **Jesus Teaches on Prayer in the Middle** 103
   Jesus came to the earth – to pray. His ministry was prayer. Out of that primary ministry came his vibrant teaching, his miraculous power, his extraordinary grace. Luke 11 is his training program in prayer.

7. **The Story of the Friend in the Middle** 117
   In this classic story, you and I are cast in the role of the intercessor – in the middle. We are placed between a hungry friend whose needs we cannot meet, and a well-supplied friend who has bread to spare! The twist? The story is constructed so that the pressure is placed on the middle position. Will the host persist in behalf of his hungry friend, even when his request is initially denied?

8. **The Prayer Principles of Jesus About the Middle.** 129
   Jesus modeled prayer. At the request of his disciples, he gave a model for prayer. Then he told an illustrative story about intercessory prayer. He then unwrapped the intercessory principles etched in the story. Though persistence is required, we are not praying to a resistant neighbor friend, Jesus reminds us, but to a caring Father – "How much more will your Father give...to those who ask persistently."

9. **Liberating the Fallen House of Adam** 143
   Jesus concludes his teaching with a story that represents a "graduate level" perception of intercession. After an exorcism, he is accused of being in a league with Satan. The story shifts. Suddenly we are no longer focused on liberating the "one" demonized man, but on liberating the "house" of Adam.

10. **Stories from the Middle**.. 179
    Here are a collage of stories about divine intervention, revival and renewal, rescue and the power of prayer in the middle.

Gandalf: *"Saruman, you missed your path in life. You should have been the king's jester and earned your bread, and stripes too. I keep a clearer memory of your arguments and deeds, than you suppose. When I last visited you, you were the jailer of Mordor, and there I was to be sent. Saruman, for the last time. Will you not come down? Isengard has proved less strong than your hope and fancy made it."*

Saruman: A shadow passed over Saruman's face; then it went deathly white. Before he could conceal it, they saw through the mask the anguish of a mind in doubt, loathing to stay and dreading to leave his refuge. For a second he hesitated, and no one breathed. Then he spoke, and his voice was shrill and cold. Pride and hate were conquering him. *"I do not trust you, Gandalf."*

Gandalf: *"The treacherous are ever distrustful. Your servants are destroyed and scattered; your neighbors you have made your enemies."*[1]

Sam Gangee: *"Well, Master, we're in a fix, and make no mistake."* Sam stood despondently with hunched shoulders. Night was gathering over the shapeless lands before them.[2]

SECTION ONE

Adam, Jesus, the Church and the Middle

Elrond: *"A part of his tale was known to some there, but the full tale to none."* Elrond told of the Elven-smiths, and their eagerness for knowledge, by which Sauron ensnared them. *"For in that time he was not yet evil to behold, and they received his aid and grew mightily in craft, and he learned their secrets and betrayed them. There was war, and the land was laid waste, and the gate of Moria was shut."* Of Numenor, he spoke, its glory and its fall, and the return of the Kings of Men to Middle-earth. *"But Sauron of Mordor assailed them, and they made the Last Alliance of Elves and Men."*

Frodo: *"I thought the fall of Gil-galad was a long time ago."*

Elrond: *"So it was indeed. But my memory reaches back to the Elder Days. I have seen three ages in the West of the world, and many defeats and many fruitless victories. Sauron himself was overthrown and Isildur cut the Ring from his hand. Sauron was diminished, but not destroyed. His Ring was lost but not unmade. The Dark Tower was broken, but its foundations were not removed."*[3]

CHAPTER ONE
ADAM: CREATED FOR THE MIDDLE

Adam and the Middle

Adam was created for the middle. He was imprinted with God's image and likeness. The Hebrew word for image, *tselem*, carries the idea of a phantom or an illusion. It suggests that the relationship intended between God and Adam was so close that Adam was designed to be God's earthly shadow. As God moved, he moved. His actions reflected, mirrored those of God. Yet a different word is used for 'likeness' – *demuth*. It means to *resemble*, even to *model*, to *behave* in a similar and like manner or pattern. Adam, and from him, the human race, was created to serve as an extension, a surrogate of God Himself.

God had breathed into him the breath of life (Genesis 2:7), to impart a nature that marked him as distinct from all creation, giving him a divine and unique spiritual component. All of creation would see him, and yet see in him and through him, the Creator.

In this middle position, he was given dominion. It was a gift. He did not have to *take* dominion, but rather to steward it. It was God's dominion, benevolently shared with him, executed through him and by him. The middle was strategic and powerful. This gift of irrevocable, strategic and singular dominion was intended for use in his servant role as the representative of God. He was over, because he was under. He was king of the earth – and yet, he was its chief servant. He was to cultivate the earth. He was a "blue-collar" regent. His role was also to guard and protect creation, including Eve. He was to be a kingly, vigilant, sentry. Through him, through the house of Adam, God would accomplish His purposes, He would establish His rule. In His blessing of Adam and his house, all the earth would be blessed. One human family, stamped with divine DNA, filling and subduing the earth with God's image – all sons of Adam. He was created for the strategic, critical middle.

Lucifer against Adam

From this place, the strategic, critical middle, Satan sought to lure him. Over the house of Adam, and the planet over which God gave him dominion, Lucifer sought control. We often juxtapose Lucifer against God. The comparison is tragically flawed. Lucifer is not God's counter opposite. Though in opposition to God, he is not an inverse equal. In fact, he is not even remotely a threat to the Divine Throne. Darkness holds no power on its own. It thrives only in the absence of light. By his mere breath, God will destroy the Evil One (2 Thessalonians 2:8). A mere angel – if an angel can be called mere – will bind Lucifer and cast him into the bottomless pit (Revelation 20:1-3). It will not even take a gang of angels. There is no contest, which by necessity involves our God in a struggle with Lucifer. God is *seated* on His throne and Lucifer's threats do not even move Him. He is not pacing heaven, wearing thin the golden streets, worriedly watching CNN to discover the next monkey-wrench that Lucifer has managed to throw into the cog-wheels of His creative and redemptive plan.

> *Lucifer is not God's counter opposite. Though in opposition to God, he is not an inverse equal. In fact, he is not remotely a threat to the Divine Throne. Darkness holds no power on its own.*

Lucifer is an enemy of God, but he is not an equal enemy. By luring Adam from the critical and strategic middle, he has gained a temporary and deadly advantage over the earth and its inhabitants. By tempting Adam to sin, our flesh-father was weakened and infected with a deadly disease. His sickness gave Lucifer opportunity. In the violence of Adam's fall, Lucifer took possession of his house. We, the children of Adam, have lived in the tyranny of this hostile takeover for millenniums. We are detainees in a house in which we were to live freely forever. Born into slavery, under the dominion of Adam's sin, we were hopelessly trapped on a planet on which we were created to live free.

We, in North America, sometimes forget that we are living on a planet which is at war with heaven. This is no small matter. In this corner of the universe, a defiant kingdom has claimed earth as home and is in rebellion against God. Lucifer is determined to establish an overtly counter kingdom here. He will be openly acknowledged and worshipped. He wills for the whole planet to defy the Creator God and to reject redemption through his Son. That

Biblical view is ignored by the mainstream of our culture and the church. Most do not even recognize the existence of Lucifer. His warfare against us has involved the use of prosperity. In other parts of the earth, we find relentless famine and disease, want and hunger, overt war and oppressive regimes which make the 'warfare' obvious. In such places, they have no difficulty seeing evil in an objective way. Here, the Evil One operates with the opposite effect. He is virtually invisible. The warfare waged against us is stealth, and it may be the most treacherous tactic Satan is using on the planet.

> *We, in North America, sometimes forget that we are living on a planet which is at war with heaven. This is no small matter.*

Here is what happened. Our ancestor, Adam, defaulted in his leadership. He was the de facto king on the earth. He was the federal head of the human race. He was the earth's priest, representing it before God. He was its prophet, charged with guarding and protecting it. He had been made a brilliant and noble creature, positioned a bit lower than the angels, crowned with glory and honor (Psalm 8:5). In his fall, everything under his power fell into the hands of the dark Lord who orchestrated the deceptive coup that led to the present occupation of the earth. All of the earth has experienced the consequences of Adam's fall. Creation groans and travails (Romans 8:25). *"In Adam, all have sinned,"* (Romans 5:12) – and tasted its consequences. In Adam, we fell under the dreadful power of an evil angel, Lucifer. He, with his demonic hosts, invisibly occupy the planet and its atmosphere. The earth is under siege (Ephesians 2:2; John 12:31; Galatians 4:3; 1 John 5:19). It is at war with heaven. And as a result of the rebellion that continues here, in which we humans are complicit, it is under the threat of judgment (Psalms 98:9; Acts 17:38).

But God, not willing that men perish (2 Peter 3:9; 2 Thessalonians 2:10) in the judgment of Lucifer and his angels, came to the earth, disguised as a man. He came as a representative of mankind to contest Lucifer's domination and to bind him, the strongman, the bully over Adam's house. Sadly, Israel did not recognize him as the Messiah warrior, the Son of David – *Mashiach ben David* (Matthew 12:23; 15:22; 20:30; 21:9; Luke 1:32; Acts 2:29-30). He was rejected by his own countrymen (John 1:11). He was crucified and buried. In that act, he fulfilled the role of *Mashiach ben Yoseph*, the rejected and suffering (Isaiah 53) son of Jacob, dead for a season, but found alive.

His blood was an investment which marked the planet for redemption. God refuses to allow Satan to dwell here permanently. A quiet revolution has begun. Raised from the dead, Jesus ascended into heaven and was seated as a man, and simultaneously as the Son of God, at the right hand of the Father (Ephesians 1:28; Hebrews 8:1). His blood sealed a new covenant between men and God, heaven and earth (Matthew 26:28; Hebrews 13:20). His acceptance at the throne put that covenant in force (Acts 2:32-33). On the basis of that covenant, those promises, and only in his name and by his blood, we now, from earth, may access the court of heaven (Romans 5:2; Hebrews 4:16). We are priviledged insiders to regular hearings in heaven's courtroom regarding the conditions on earth. We have the assurance that an intervention is planned, without which, we are helplessly trapped by the escalating global dimensions of Lucifer's acceptance here.[4]

Lucifer's contest for the earth is formidable. He is defeated, but he refuses to surrender. He bears a deadly wound, and is now fighting with an angry disposition (Revelation 13:3). He is convinced that he can revive himself, defy death and captivity; that he can recover from the death blow of the resurrection and ascension. He is deluded, but still he moves violently through the earth

(1 Peter 5:8; Revelation 2:10; 12:12). How chilling it must have been for him, to have realized after the death of Christ, that he had been complicit in the sacrifice of the first perfect human, the first sinless life, the perfect redemptive offering (Hebrews 4:15). Now, that man, Jesus, is in heaven. He is the ultimate first fruit (Revelation 1:5), the head of a new race of mortals, of humans, who in intensifying numbers are gathering to God as their Father. Jesus is the King of the earth, though though he now reigns. He is still the only true heir to the throne of David (Acts 2) and redeemer of the fallen house of Adam. He now serves as an intercessor (Romans 8:34) for all of creation, particularly for the redeemed. Lucifer knows this. Prayer is his daily nemesis, the deadly connection between the bride-Church and the bridegroom, Christ. For this reason, Lucifer is mad, and more determined than ever.

> GALADRIEL: The power of the enemy is growing. Sauron will use his puppet Saruman to destroy the people of Rohan. Isengard has been unleashed. The Eye of Sauron now turns to Gondor, the last free kingdom of men. His war on this country will come swiftly. In the gathering dark...
>
> Men, who are so easily seduced... Sauron will have dominion over all life on this Earth, even unto the ending of the world. The time of the elves is over. Do we leave Middle-Earth to its fate? Do we let them stand alone?[5]

Like a caged animal, he continues to hold the earth hostage (Daniel 7:17-22; Revelation 13:1-9). It is no longer God's heavenly throne to which he aspires. Even in his delusional state, he recognizes that as an impossible reach as a consequence of the failed angelic rebellion (Isaiah 14:12-16). So in Genesis, he reached for a lower, yet still exalted prize – the dominion and representative authority of Adam, over the earth. Here, he is still determined to be worshipped. Here, he is still resolute to establish his illegal kingdom. It will eventually fail. Christ will appear and claim the kingdoms of this world as his own.

Lucifer is formidable. At least, he is still a powerful enemy to mortals (Ephesians 6:12), but we must cease seeing Lucifer as the polar and equal opposite of God, as if he is comparable. *In opposition* to God? Yes, madly so. But *an opposite* to God, rationally comparable in power or authority – *No!* At some point in the unwrapping of the eschatological calendar, we will be allowed to pay our twenty-five cents and get a first-hand view of the hand-cuffed adversary of righteousness as he is carted away for trial. Isaiah anticipates the moment,

> *Those who see you [Lucifer] will gaze at you, and consider you, saying: 'Is this the man [one] who made the earth tremble, Who shook kingdoms, Who made the world as a wilderness and destroyed its cities, who did not open the house of his prisoners?'* (Isaiah 14:16-17).

What a smoke and mirror show! Distorted theology has rendered Lucifer larger and God smaller. That perception is flawed. The moon in an eclipse appears to block the sun, but if we were to assume it to be the same size, we would make a great mistake. In fact, the moon is only 2,160 miles in diameter, smaller and lighter than earth. The sun is 864,000 miles in diameter, 400 times larger than the moon. The eclipse of the sun by the moon is an optical illusion that gives birth to unfounded notions. Satan's seeming ability to block out truth's light does the same. It gives cause for men not to believe in the existence of God. He has disappeared. He is not apparent. Thus, we must have evolved, and faith is only mythology. It is all a part of Lucifer's deceptive scheme.

The theological distortion also affects our view of man. Adam was a much more noble and powerful creature than our current view of him (Psalms 4-6). Science teaches evolution. The Bible teaches devolution – a fall. Sin caused an incredible and irreversible downward tumble. Do we realize how far we fell? We see the sin of Adam as resulting in a scratch on his knee and a skinned elbow. He got caught stealing apples off of his divine neighbor's tree. Not a really bad thing. What damage could result from such a benign moral act? Our view makes little distinction between Adam after the fall or before – perhaps he was a bit more innocent, uninitiated and without guilt for some brief period. We are wrong. We have grossly underestimated the damage that sin did to the noble creature Adam, and to his seed, mankind.

He was identified with God. We now identify with the animal kingdom, and so much so that our society is convinced, deluded into believing that we evolved, that we are graduated primates. Adam was a splendid creature who carried the image of God (Genesis 1:27; Romans 8:29; 1 Corinthians 15:49; 2 Corinthians 3:18). He was more divine than earthly. He was a spirit being with a body, not merely a body with a spiritual dimension. Flawless. Sinless. Gallant. Having dominion. He was an aristocrat and a farmer. He was given the privilege of naming the animals (Genesis 2:19-20), which implies a com-

> *Adam was a splendid creature who carried the image of God... more divine than earthly...a spirit being with a body... Flawless. Sinless. Gallant. Having dominion. His position was so exalted, his scepter so dominant, his reign so reaching, his capacity for multiplication and fruitfulness so exponential, that Lucifer desired it.*

manding and watchful role. He was given the charge of guarding the garden, a protective role. He walked with God and was thereby invited into divine fellowship. The whole earth was his and that of his heirs as a gift. The whole earth was his and Eve's to protect and guard. His position was so exalted, his scepter so dominant, his reign so reaching, his capacity for multiplication and fruitfulness so exponential, that Lucifer desired it.

If Lucifer could not dethrone God in His heaven (Isaiah 14:13-15); if he could not have God's role, he would have man's role. If he could not be God, he would take His 'image' hostage. Without the capacity to create, he can only steal. This has become his *modus operandi* through history (John 10:10; Luke 4:6; John 8:44). He seeks to steal thrones. When Yahweh's throne proved far from his reach, he grasped for Adam's representative throne. When Christ came to the earth, he pretended that he had a throne to give. "*All this* [the kingdoms of the world] *I will give you,*" he said, "*if you will bow down and worship me*" (Matthew 4:9). The deed he offered was fraudulent. The throne he will offer the Anti-Christ will be without a foundation. His style is to steal, and substitute.

The great villains of the Old Testament did the same – Cain substituted false worship for the true (Genesis 4:3-5; Hebrews 11:4; Jude 1:11). Balaam substituted a false prophecy for the truth (Numbers 22:24; Deuteronomy 23:4-5; 2 Peter 2:15). Korah sought an expansion of his role, a greater sphere of authority to which he was not entitled (Numbers 16:19-49; Jude 1:11).

Without the ability to give life, Lucifer's substitute reign is sadly destined to infuse anything in his shadow with death. Without the character that edifies, he destroys all he takes to himself (John 10:10). And yet, with the earth so fully alive, so vibrant with energy, so marked with the fingerprints of God, there is still much life force here, even after the fall, enough for him to hijack for evil purposes.

While Lucifer was no match for Yahweh, he proved more than a match for Adam. It did not have to be that way. Adam fell by the exercise of his own free will (Romans 5:12, 14; 12:14), through the power of Lucifer's deadly deception, as did Eve (2 Corinthians 11:13). In Adam's fall, his family, the whole line of humanity, has come under this deceptive power. Consequently, we are under Lucifer's brutal tyranny.

> SAM: Do you remember the Shire, Mr. Frodo? It'll be spring soon. And the orchards will be in blossom. And the birds will be nesting in the hazel thicket. And they'll be sowing the summer barley in the lower fields... and eating the first of the strawberries with cream. Do you remember the taste of strawberries?[6]

In Adam's fallen condition, weak and sin-sick, neither he nor his sons had the moral authority or the power to revolt and regain control of his house. Cain, his oldest son, would adopt the behavioral profile of the tyrant Lucifer. He would become the world's first assassin (Genesis 4:8). Lucifer became the earth's alternative irresponsible father figure (John 8:44, 49). Cain would murder his own righteous brother, Abel (1 John 3:12). Lucifer would begin through Cain, the long war of the unrighteous on the righteous, earning Cain a place among Jude's trio of three legendary Old Testament villains (Jude 11). He would rail against true and pure worship, styling worship to suit himself. Rejected and unapproved by God, his anger would move him into a murderous rage to destroy his brother. Adam's house, in one generation, erupted into civil war. It is still under siege and his sons are still at war with one another. In such chaos, Lucifer is at his best.

The Siege of Adam's House

Adam would eventually die as a hostage in his own house, shut out of the beautiful garden and separated from his Creator by sin and sin's terrible reign. Lucifer would watch generations come and go, until the whole house of Adam and the entire earth was populated. He and his invisible rebel angel occupiers would hold the earth and its resident's hostage. Bloody empire after empire would rise, all energized to some degree by Lucifer (Revelation 13:1; Daniel 7). Under the bondage of sin and death, mankind had no remedy to throw off the tyranny. It had no cure for the soul sickness and the social disease that came with sin. Death smothered life.

Lucifer would settle in above the earth, in the middle heaven (Ephesians 2:2; Luke. 10:18). From that place, he has orchestrated havoc with the order of creation and among its creatures, particularly man. He had wanted a seat beside God (Isaiah 14:13), and failing to grasp that undeserved honor, he rebelled and led a coup involving as many as a third of the angels in heaven (Revelation 12:4, 7, 9). As a consolation prize, he seized measured control over the earth and the seat of Adam. He is the *"god of this world"* (2 Corinthians 4:4) but he is neither my God nor yours. He is the god of a system that the Scripture calls "the world" (John 12:25, 31; 46-47; 2 Timothy 4:10; Titus 2:2; James 1:27; 4:4 2 Peter 2:20). It is out of control, polluted by sin and separated from God by the loss of the middle connector, the defeat of its human servant-king, Adam.

Over this earth, Lucifer has declared himself to be earth's god and king. He operates from the middle heaven (Ephesians 2:2), attempting to eclipse the earth's view of God. He whispers that, "it all evolved." He knows that if our Creation-Fall narrative is rejected, we have no understanding of who and whose we are, or of the fall of man; no basis for understanding evil and no need for a redeemer. He denies the very existence of God, but specifically His roles as Creator and Redeemer (Romans 1:19-20). "You are all alone," he tells us. Though he has been content with anonymity, that will not continue. He wants to be worshipped (Revelation 13:2-4).

He will eventually install his own false prophet, his own "christ" whom he will anoint. Thus, he will have his own "Adam," his own prototypical human. He will convince many inhabitants on the earth (Revelation 16:12-14; 13:1-8), that he is the savior of the planet. Jesus and his followers will be viewed as villains. He will look like a lamb and speak like a dragon (Revelation 13:1-10). He has been working from the time of the fall of the first Adam to establish his own kingdom on the earth and to be worshipped by mankind (Matthew 4:8-10). As always, he promises what he cannot deliver, what, in fact, is not even his own. He is peddling stolen goods – the earth itself, and its kingdoms, nations, and people groups.

> *Our purpose here, however, is not warfare. It is the reconciliation of man to God and God to man by a salvation relationship.*

As he continues to occupy the high ground of the contested middle, his war continues. This critical, strategic, uncomfortable, and sometimes bloody middle is the ground of intercession, to which we have been assigned. Our purpose here, however, is not warfare. It is the reconciliation of man to God and God to man by a salvation relationship. As intercessors, we have jurisdiction in this critical and utterly indispensable communication post between heaven and earth. It is an assignment in illegally occupied territory. So, our base of operation is often under fire. We pray in a war zone. Intercession is the call to 'watch on the wall,' the place between in-and-out, saved and lost, good and evil, right and wrong, the kingdom of God and the kind of darkness; the place between whole and broken, between what was and what is, and also, between what is about to be, indeed, what will be. Warfare is not the heart of our intercessory calling. We proclaim good news in a bad news world; we offer hope; we bind up the broken-hearted, we set captives free, we open prison doors; we declare the coming day of Jubliee.

Under fire, it is far too easy to forget that our primary role is to keep earth-to-heaven communication channels open. At times, it is necessary to return enemy fire, but always remembering that we must quickly return to the conciliatory dimension of prayer, to pure intercession. Under no conditions can the middle be surrendered. The vacancy of the middle has dire consequences. The desire of God is that prayer is ceaselessly offered in every place, the communication channels open 24-7. If intercession ceases, if the connection between heaven and earth is broken, our work is immobilized. Prayer is our only hope, not only because of the power that flows through prayer, but because it is the means by which the authority of Jesus, heaven's intercessor, earth's rightful king is conveyed. As we agree with him in prayer, he is also praying to the Father for us. He is then passing to us heaven's intelligence information on the state of our mission. He will direct our paths. He will order our steps. He will send angelic reinforcements. He is, by the Spirit, with us. He, in prayer, comes to us. And in the end, he will come for us!

---

1 Tolkien, *The Lord of the Rings: The Two Towers*, 206-207.
2 Ibid, 231.
3 Tolkien, *The Lord of the Rings: The Fellowship of the Ring*, 272-273. A free paraphrase.
4 See the teaching series: *Heaven Is A Courtroom*, by P. Douglas Small, available from Alive Ministries.
5 Tolkien, *The Lord of the Rings: The Two Towers*.
6 Tolkien, *The Lord of the Rings: The Return of the King*.

Discussion Guide

1. Discuss Adam's creation role, his position in the middle as a model and pattern for all his sons, including us. Talk about his dominion – his charge to cultivate and guard the garden. What does this creation order imply regarding our role?
2. Talk about Lucifer (the Devil, the Serpent, Satan) – a comparable opposite of God? Or an incomparable opponent in delusional opposition? Do you think we overrate Lucifer's powers?
3. Discuss the concept of 'Adam's house' and the human race as his family, his descendents. Draw an analogy between inherited and flawed DNA, predispositions to this disease or that – and the sin principle.
4. With Alex Haley's classic book and film series, *Roots,* as a backdrop, discuss what it would be like to be born the child of a slave – entrapped in a political, social and economic system from which there was no escape for you or your children. The Bible uses this analogy for us and the whole world – we were born as slaves. Do you think the freedoms and blessings of our culture blind us to such a fact?
5. Jesus came – not as a son of Adam, but virgin born, to liberate Adam's enslaved house. With his blood, he redeemed the planet he had been instrumental in creating (Colossians 1:16; John 1:3). He is the last Adam, creating a new line, a new race of men (Ephesians 2:15; Galatians 3:28; Colossians 3:10-11). What are the implications of such ideas?
6. How do we, the bride, partner with Jesus to complete his work?
7. Discuss the fall of man. What was man like before the fall (a little lower than angels), and then, after the fall? How far did man fall? Did Jesus come to show us what God was like? Were his works a demonstration of what man was originally capable of?
8. How important is the creation-fall narrative to our understanding of both redemption and mission?
9. Lucifer will establish his own kingdom in the earth – political, social and spiritual. Why, in the face of the resurrection and

ascension, the descent of the Spirit and the enthronement of Jesus in the heavens, is Satan so delusion and determined? Why does the church lack equal rational resolve?

10. Discuss Lucifer's occupation of the 'middle heaven' and what that means. He is the 'prince of the power of the air' – what does that mean?

Gimli: *"The world was fair, the mountains tall in Elder Days before the Fall."* [1]

Saruman: *"Do you know how the Orcs first came to be? They were elves first, taken by the dark powers, a ruined and terrible form of life, and now perfected. My fighting force."*

Who do you serve? The Orcs roared, "Saruman!"

Aragorn: *"We should leave now. The Orcs patrol the eastern shore."*

Legolas: *"It is not the eastern shore that worries me. A shadow and threat has been growing in my mind. Something draws near. I can feel it…"*

Frodo: *"I wish the ring had never come to me. I wish none of this had happened."*

Gandalf: *"So do all who live to see such times. But that is not theirs to decide."*

CHAPTER TWO
JESUS RECLAIMS THE MIDDLE

Jesus Secures the Middle

The Old Testament is a record of the flashes of God's light and revelation in the darkness, of godly men and women who quietly, and some boldly, defied the tyranny. It is a record of triumphs and tragedies, of judgment and redemption. Prophets boldly declared the existence of God and called men to repent. Deliverers rose up and threw off oppression. But none were able to break the ultimate power of Lucifer's hold on the earth. None were able to offer a tonic to cure the deadly disease that caused Adam's children to continue to die in every generation – the deadly disease of sin (1 Corinthians 15:22). Prophets called men and women with sensitive hearts back to righteous paths. Priests pointed the way to reconciliation, but the altar over which they presided could offer only a temporary cure.

Jesus Comes to Adam's House

The writer of Hebrews declares that, *"God at various times and in various ways spoke"* (Hebrews 1:1). The New American Standard says, He spoke *"in many portions and in many ways."* Piecemeal – in bits and pieces, the truth broke forth. But, then God spoke again, in one final and compelling way. *"In these last days [He has] spoken to us by His Son, whom He has appointed heir of all things, through whom also He made the worlds"* (Hebrews 1:2). Jesus is God's final word. And he is no mere mortal. He mediated life itself. *"Through whom (Christ, the Word) also He, (God, the Father), made the worlds"* (Hebrews 1:2; 11:3; Colossians 1:16). The One we know as Jesus has always been in the middle. He, as the Word, was in the middle of creation. And now, he is in the middle of redemption (Ephesians 2:14; Colossians 1:20). There is no authentic access to the One and only true God, than through the mediator, Jesus, the Christ, the Lord. 1 Timothy 2:5 declares, *"For there is one God and one mediator between God and men, the man Christ Jesus."* Hebrews 9:15 declares, Christ is the mediator of a new covenant (testament), that those who are called may receive the promised eternal inheritance – now that he has died as a ransom to set them free from the sins committed under the first covenant (Old Testament).

In the fullness of time, God, the Father, sent Jesus (Galatians 4:4). He was born of woman, but he was no mere mortal. He was not a son of Adam (Matthew 1:23; Luke. 1:27). He was *Mashiach ben Jossef*, the suffering and displaced Son. He was simultaneously, *Mashiach ben David*, the warring and kingly son. He was God's Son – human and divine, mortal and eternal, flesh and spirit. He was man and he was God. He was tempted, but without sin. He felt pain, and he healed its source. He was crucified with a crown of thorns, but nevertheless, crowned. He was lamb and lion (Revelation 5:4-6). He suffered, and in doing so, he conquered. He was *"Word become flesh"* (John 1:1). He was *"with God, and he was God."* He was not *a* word, but *'The'* Word. Not a prophet, but *'The' Prophet.* John makes it clear, as does the writer of Hebrews, that he was there from the beginning, a mediator in the Creation event itself. *"All things were made through Him, and without Him nothing that was made that was made"* (John 1:3). He was the source of life (1:4). *"He came to his own, and his own received him not, but to those who received them, he gave power to become the sons of God"* (John 1:11-12). He was the light that shown in the darkness, even though the darkness did not comprehend it.

> *There are two corporate men on the earth – Adam and Christ. We are born into Adam, and we must die and be born again to be planted in the body of Christ. Baptism is the symbolic act that transfers us from the old man (Adam) to the new man (Christ).*

The Body of Adam and the Body of Christ

All are descended from Adam and all are born into and under his judgment (Romans 5:12) – except for one, Jesus. He was not a son of Adam. He was, by the Holy Spirit, the Seed of God. There are two corporate men – Adam and Jesus, the Christ (1 Corinthians 15:22). We are born into Adam, under slavery to sin and its penalty death. At the cross, we choose, by grace, to die – to sin and self. We renounce sin. We switch sides. We are baptized, buried alive, and born again. Raised to new life, we are transferred from the corporate body of Adam, planted into the body of Christ

(John. 3:3-8; 1 Peter 1:23).

Baptism is the public sign, the powerful, symbolic act that demonstrates our liberation from the old man (Adam) to the new man, Christ (1 Corinthians 12:13; Galatians 3:27; Romans 6:3-5). In Adam, we die.

> From the ashes a fire shall be woken, A light from the shadows shall spring; Renewed shall be the blade that was broken: The crownless again shall be king.[2]

In Christ, we are made alive. Adam – the unredeemed corporate mass of humanity – is dying. The body of Christ – the new corporate man – comprised of individual believers (members) is being renewed (2 Corinthians 4:16; Ephesians 5:30). Adam is energized by the fleshly dimension, and by hell itself (Ephesians 2:1-3; 4:22). The body of Christ is energized by the Holy Spirit.

Every man born on the earth, but one, has come into the world as a son of Adam (Luke 1:27, 34-37). Jesus, however, was no son of Adam. He was the Son of God (John 1:1-16). This is why the virgin birth is such an important teaching. If Jesus was born of Adam, he was born in sin and as a slave - and therefore, he could not have saved us. If a sinner, any sinner, even a noble sinner, could save himself, there would be no absolute need for divine intervention, no need for a Savior for all men (Leviticus 4:3; John 8:7; Hebrews 4:15). But, in truth, all men need to be saved, there was and is no alternative. The virgin birth, the sinless life and the subsequent death of the innocent Jesus is rendered meaningless if all men did not need a savior, a redeemer and a deliverer (John 3:17; 1 Timothy 1:15). If some could save themselves, or if there were other paths, then Jesus only offers one additional way among many ways. That renders his death as senseless. And the Father's role in his incarnation and the crucifixion as cruel at best. Such a scenario fails to see the hopelessly desperate plight of humanity. There was and is no other way. All but one have descended from Adam. Jesus came as the Trojan baby – slipping into the earth under Lucifer's radar screen. For years, he had been destroying potential infant deliverers. He tried to destroy this one as well (Matthew 2:16; Exodus 1:22; 2:1-8; Jeremiah 31:15; Matthew 2:18), but he failed.

Jesus came as the last Adam, not the second or the third, but the last (1 Corinthians 15:45; Romans 5:11-13). He came to end Adam's line for all who would receive him (John 1:12). He came to end the tyranny (1 John 3:8; Hebrews 2:14). He came to throw off the rebellion of Lucifer (Hebrews 2:8; 1 Corinthians 15:25-27; Romans 16:20), to open our eyes to the invisible siege that holds mankind hostage (Isaiah 42:7; Acts 26:17-19). He came to Adam's house to bind the strongman, Lucifer, and liberate the house (Matthew 12:29; Mark 3:27) from the tyranny of sin and death. It is what he announced,

> *The Spirit of the Lord is upon me, because He has anointed Me to preach the gospel to the poor; He has sent Me to heal the brokenhearted, to proclaim liberty to the captives and recovery of sight to the blind, to set at liberty those who are oppressed; to proclaim the acceptable year of the LORD* (Luke 4:18-19).

His mission was more than the healing of the wounded in the house of Adam or a mere proclamation of hope. His mission was not merely an ideological revolution, nor is ours. It was a revolt against the tyranny of an unseen Evil Despot. He came to liberate Adam's house. Matthew 12:29, *"How can one enter a strong man's house and plunder his goods, unless he first binds the strong man? And then he will plunder his house."* God's ways are not our ways. It was in surrender that He surmounted. It was in embracing our sin, though He knew no sin, that He destroyed its power. It was by tasting death, that He proved it powerless over holiness.

Crucified, he, unlike any other man before him, swallowed death rather than having death swallow him (Isaiah 25:8; 1 Corinthians 15:55-56). He entered hell's tomb, the grave, not as a prisoner, but as a liberator (Ephesians 4:8-9; 1 Peter 4:6; 3:18-19). He emancipated those in the prison house of death who had died awaiting his coming. He moved paradise to better quarters. In his ascension, he presented himself to heaven as the son of Joseph and the son of David, the suffering and triumph Messiah, rolled into one. He assumed David's throne (Luke 1:32; Acts 2:29-36).

The Last Adam – Enthroned

Peter declared, *"the patriarch David...is both dead and buried, and his tomb is with us to this day"* (Acts 2:30). And yet, it was from the root of David that the Messiah would come and establish an everlasting throne. David, being a *"prophet, and knowing that God had sworn with an oath to him that of the fruit of his body, according to the flesh, He would raise up the Christ to sit on his throne"* (2:31). Peter declared this to be a prophecy of *"the resurrection of the Christ, that His soul was not left in Hades, nor did His flesh see corruption"* (2:32).

David's throne is now occupied, but it is not a resurrected David that sits on it, but *"this Jesus"* whom *"God has raised up, of which we are all witnesses"* (2:33). David, through his seed, by Mary, is back on the throne, though not on earth. He has been *"exalted to the right hand of God."* He is ruling his kingdom in exile. The proof of this is the descent and infilling of the Spirit. A new class and calling of priests has now been inaugurated. With the outpouring of the Holy Spirit on the Day of Pentecost, they participated in the coronation of the new King of the earth and his installation as High Priest of heaven's tabernacle. And they have *"received from the Father the promise of the Holy Spirit, He poured* out this which you now see and hear" (Acts 2:33).

"David," Peter said boldly "did not ascend into the heavens." His grave is still visible to all in Jerusalem. But one in his line has been counted worthy to ascend to his throne. The Father, *"The LORD,"* Yahweh, *"said to my Lord,"* a reference to Jesus, *"Sit at My right hand, till I make Your enemies Your footstool"* (Matthew 22:24; Hebrews 1:13; Acts 2:25-35). His words are staggering. We

> *David's throne is now occupied... Christ is ruling from a kingdom in exile... We have a human in heaven - a man! Jesus, stands there, having endured the test of death itself, He overcame. He holds the keys to hell and the grave.*

have a human in heaven – a man! And yet no mere mortal. The abandoned and contested middle has been secured for eternity. A flawless man, Jesus, stands there. He resisted temptation. He endured the test of death itself, and overcame. He holds the keys to hell. He is God, and he is also man. *"Therefore let all the house of Israel know assuredly that God has made this Jesus, whom you crucified, both Lord and Christ"* (Acts 2:36).

David's throne is now and will be forever filled. Pentecost was the confirmation that heaven had installed Jesus as the new High Priest of heaven's tabernacle after the order of Melchizedek (Hebrews 7:17). Heaven held his coronation. He is king, not only of Israel, but the King of kings, the King of the earth, standing in the stead of Adam. He is now enthroned in exile (Acts 2:31-36; Ephesians 1:22; Hebrews 2:8). His kingdom is disputed here, but not in heaven, and not here among his followers, not by his bride-partner. We are the under-cover operatives of his exiled kingdom, working along the edges of the darkness, whispering hope into the shadows, sharing the news that Jesus is not dead, that he is alive.

The Church – A Kingdom Agent

We are now agents of the "not yet fully come" kingdom. *"The Kingdom of God is at hand,"* Jesus declared (Matthew 3:2; 10:7). It is here - and yet, it has not-yet-fully-come. He came, and was rejected here. But heaven has accepted him and affirmed his coming to earth. With his blood, he redeemed those of the lost family of Adam who will receive him and declare him Lord. With his death, he answered sin's penalty. With his perfect and sinless life, he did what the first Adam did not do. He said a resounding "No!" to Lucifer. Temptation could not seduce. And the pressure and trial of the cross could not deter him.

It was not the Creator's design that had caused the first fall, that was clear now. It was not the fault of God that the first Adam fell. It was human error. And with that made clear, hell had no claim on Christ, only on sin. And sin, though found *on* him, was not *in* him (Hebrews 4:15; 2 Corinthians 5:21). With my sin and yours imputed to him, he took our sin to the grave, to hell, in order that we might not be pulled into that vortex of judgment by our own sin (Romans 5:12-14). Not if we cry out to him for salvation. Not if we embrace the cross, renounce sin, and confess Jesus as Savior.

By Adam's sin, one man's disobedience, the federal head of the human race, the reigns of the earth had been seized by the Evil One, Satan. Sin had given him occasion. And now by one man's obedience, Jesus, the head of a new race of men, a new corporate body, Adam's scepter has been recovered. *"All authority is given to Me in heaven and in earth"* (Matthew 18:18; John 17:2), he would declare. The throne of mankind has been recovered. Heaven and earth, God and man, are no longer separated (Romans 5:10; 2 Corinthians 5:18-20).

Paul declared that, *"by Him all things consist"* (Colossians

1:17), that is – all things are held together. Jesus is the ultimate bond. He is and will forever be "in the middle." He ever lives to make intercession for us (Hebrews 7:25). He is the bridegroom, and we are his Church, the partner-bride (Matthew 9:15; 25; Ephesians 5:25). He operates on heaven's side, between God, the Father, and His Church, reaching through them as yeilded instruments and annointed vessels, to unsaved mankind. We operate on earth's side, standing with him, agreeing with him as his visible partners, but also in the middle, reaching upward in behalf of lost family and friends, praying for the restoration of all things (Acts 3:20-22). He is on the upper-side of the middle – the ultimate intercessor. We are on the lower-side of the middle – partners in intercession and mission with him.

We are called to the middle – the uncomfortable, critical, strategic, often bloody, middle.

---

1 Tolkien, *The Lord of the Rings: The Two Towers* (Book Two, Chapter 4). See also, Kurt Bruner and Jim Ware, *Finding God in The Lord of the Rings* (Wheaton, IL: Tyndale, 2001), 1. A free paraphrase.
2 Tolkien, *The Lord of the Rings: The Fellowship of the Ring.*

Discussion Guide

1. Jesus is God's final word. God, in Christ, came to the earth. There can be no clearer message – yet, the earth is still in rebellion. Why?

2. Jesus is the mediator between heaven and earth. What does that mean?

3. How important is it that Jesus was the key heavenly agent of both creation and redemption? Suppose God created us and the world, but had not chosen to redeem us? What are the implications? Suppose He is our Redeemer, but not our Creator? Who made us? Whose image do we bear? Does it matter? What right did He have to redeem what was never His?

4. Talk about the two corporate men – Adam and Christ. You have probably heard the term, "the body of Christ." But did you know Adam also had a body? We were born in Adam. How do we get out of the old man, Adam, and into the new man, Christ?

5. Peter declared that Jesus was seated on David's throne. He is ruling. He is the King, not only of Israel, but of the earth. He is now reigning in exile. What does that mean for us?

6. John the Baptist, Jesus and Peter, preached on the Kingdom. Both the gospels and Acts, open and close with notes on the Kingdom. We are agents of 'the Kingdom of God' which is 'at hand.' Do you agree?

7. The kingdom has come! But it has "not yet fully come." We are living in the era between kingdoms. We seek the Kingdom of God. We preach the Lordship of Christ. We live by kingdom principles. We operate in kingdom authority with flashes of kingdom power.

8. Adam was given 'all authority' and we are given similar authority. Discuss the similarities between Gen. 1:28 and the Great Commission.

9. Jesus is the High Priest in heaven - of heaven's Tabernacle. We worship in heavenly places, experiencing the presence of God through Christ. He blesses us and our labor. He completes his work through us.

10. Jesus operates on heaven's side, and we, on earth's side, but both in the middle. We are agents of heaven, partners with Jesus in prayer and mission. What are the implications of such a partnership?

DENETHOR, THE OLD MAN: *"Dark indeed is the hour, and at times you are wont to come…though all the signs forebode that the doom is drawing nigh. It has been told me that you bring with you who saw my son die. Is this he?"*

GANDALF: *"It is. One of twain. The other may come hereafter. Be not unjust in your grief. Boromir claimed the errand and would not suffer anyone else to have it. He was a masterful man."* [1]

PIPEN: *"The mightiest man may be slain by one arrow, and Boromir was pierced by many. He was very valiant."* [2]

DENETHOR TO PIPPEN: *"I see that strange tales are woven about you, and once again it is shown that looks may belie the man."* [3]

GANDALF TO PIPPEN: *"Remember that! For you are now sworn to his service. I do not know what put it into your head, or your heart, to do that. But it was well done. I did not hinder it, for generous deed should not be checked by cold counsel. You are at his command; and he will not forget."* [4]

CHAPTER THREE
MANKIND AND THE REDEMPTIVE MIDDLE

Man and the Redemptive Middle

Standing at the foot of the cross, we experience an incredible miracle – we are separated from our sin (Hebrews 10:10-12; 1 John 3:5). Its power and hold over us is rendered dead, and we are liberated from the grip of its penalty. The cancer rolls off, and we miraculously live. Like the undeserving Roman soldier who left the cross wearing the seamless robe of Christ (John 19:23-25), we walk away, former sinners, now wrapped in the ultimate robe of righteousness. Clothed with a divine wrap, we are wearing the cloak of Jesus. Imagine how heaven views us! We are wearing his "hand-me-down!" Elijah's mantle was an incredibly powerful gift to Elisha (2 Kings 2:14). But it cannot compare with the significance of the invisible robe in which every believer is wrapped, who stands repenting at the foot of the cross (Isaiah 61:10; Psalms 132:10; Romans 5:17). Heaven sees and rejoices. Hell sees and knows it has no condemnation to counter such grace and liberty (Ephesians 6:14).

The Redemptive Middle

Christ came, as the last Adam, to restore the middle. There could never be another. He was the Father's only Son (1 John 4:9). This was not the task of an angel. The creation had fallen captive. The Creator alone could redeem it. He came not from a position of power, but of service. Not as a conquering deity, but as a mortal man (Philippians 2:6-11). Not with immunity from failure, but with a vulnerability to temptation as Adam had in the beginning – the freedom of choice (Hebrews 4:15).

On his back were placed all of our chances to escape the terrible reign of sin and death, and to overthrow the illegitimate and illegal tyranny of Lucifer's siege. It was heaven's gamble. And it worked. He succeeded. He triumphed. Born of a virgin, like a Trojan-baby, he came into the earth under the radar screen of the Evil One. He conquered death, by surrendering to it. He overcame, as a servant. He met hate with love. He did not seek power; he shunned attempts to make him king by sinful human hands. He *"counted equality with God"* a thing not to be grasped (Philippians 2:5). He did not seize power – even the power and privilege of divinity. Rather, he *"emptied Himself, taking the form of a servant, being made in the likeness of men; but made Himself of no reputation"* (Philippians 2:6-7). He did not even seek to make a name for himself (Philippians 2:7). And in doing so, He has a name that, though the world wars against it, cannot be extinguished. *"He humbled Himself and became obedient to the point of death, even the death of the cross"* (Philippians 2:8).

> *God also has highly exalted Him and given Him the name which is above every name, that at the name of Jesus every*

knee should bow, of those in heaven, and of those on earth, and of those under the earth, and that every tongue should confess that Jesus Christ is Lord, to the glory of God the Father (Phil. 2:9-11).

We are, by salvation, transitioned from the body of Adam to the body of Christ. Moved from the old man into the new man, we have been baptized into his body (1 Corinthians 12:13). We have a new head for the human race (Ephesians 4:14-16). To those who no longer want to cooperate with sin and death, with transgression and tyranny, we offer the Kingship of Christ.

Our Redemptive Mission

Our goal is to enable the transfer of men out of the body of Adam, the dying corporate mass, energized by dark powers (Ephesians 2:2) into the living body of Christ, through the miracle of the new birth.

We now facilitate flashes of light in the darkness, signs and wonders, meant to call attention to the reality of the unseen, invisible kingdom. We declare that Jesus is not dead, he is alive. He is physically away, but through the agency of the Holy Spirit, he is spiritually present. He is on a mission to prepare a place for us, securing our redemption in heaven, but we have neither been left alone or powerless (John 14:19, 25f). We have been given authority in his physical absence. We are his bride partner; our bridegroom is not dead. We are not a widow. In his name, we do the works that he did, to reveal his resurrection life (John 14:12). We do so, not to call attention to ourselves, but to his reality, to his Kingdom. Listen to the whispers in the slave camps – a liberator has come to the planet. A new Kingdom is breaking in. He has gone away, but the return of the King is certain and the defeat of the dark powers assured. Join the revolution.

He came to the earth, to re-secure the middle, and, therefore, he was destined for the middle cross. There, he split humanity in half, with belief on one side and unbelief on the other. He calls us now to hold the re-secured middle. In heaven, he will serve to connect men to God, reconciling them, forgiving sin and forging a new friendship, with the Creator Father. He calls us his bride-partner, to join him from earth in that role.

> The Nameless Enemy has arisen again. Smoke rises once more from Orodruin that we call Mount Doom. The power of the Black Land grows and we are hard beset. When the Enemy returned our folk were driven from Ithilien, our fair domain... Sudden war came upon us out of Mordor, and we were swept away. We were outnumbered, but it was not by numbers that we were defeated. A power was there that we had not felt before.[5]

Every temptation is the attempt on the part of Lucifer to lure us from the strategic middle. Every trial and test is an attempt to drive us from the strategic middle. Here in the middle connector role, we touch heaven through our relationship with Christ and bring it to the earth. *"Thy kingdom come! Thy will be done."* Here, we bring earth to heaven through priestly intercession. It is precisely to this middle role that we have been called, and it is on the bloody and contested ground of the middle, where the sacred right of intercession for others has been won in our behalf.

The Problem of an Abandoned Middle

Any temptation to which we submit, that distracts us and draws us away from the holy and sacred ground of the middle, can be forgiven by God's grace. It can be cleansed and removed by the redemptive blood. But the *kairos* distraction that took us out of service momentarily, that created the dissonant disconnect between us and God, in our role as an intercessor – that moment may be missed forever. Our sins do separate us from God. Out of service, distracted, the connection is momentarily lost. Like static on a screen, whatever stream of grace we were projecting, whatever river of spiritual energy was flowing through our intercessory role, is – if only for the hour or day – disrupted. And such separation has consequences far beyond us, just as Adam's separation still affects the earth.

Too often pastors fall. They are victims of the effective warfare being waged against the church to dislodge it from some strategic middle, to make it powerless, so the nation can be claimed by the Evil One. Another pastor is appointed after some tragic fall by his beloved predecessor. The church services will continue. The church will not close its doors, and yet, the violations to trust, and the damage to credibility, are like a wound for which only grace and time are cures.

> *Whenever prayer becomes decidedly about us - God stops answering.*

Meanwhile, flickers of darkness obscure the light. Innocent lambs are wounded. Relationship connections, critical to kingdom development, are severed. The damage can only be understood by gazing at the cross.

While the fall of a trusted leader may give up some strategic middle ground, in the same way, the steadfast refusal of Jesus to give place to any attitude or action, any sin or transgression, that would allow a separation between he and the Father, now facilitates the healing and conciliatory process. Connections on earth's side will fail. But the connection on heaven's side will never fail. Men will fall. One man did not – and he remains faithful now.

The trial, with exacting pressure, that mounts until our nerves are frayed and our emotions are on edge, our coffers empty and our cupboards bare, our energy sapped and hope diminished – all that pressure is aimed at getting us to abandon our post for a softer assignment. Having left some uncomfortable middle for relief, a critical life-giving connection is sometimes broken. Kingdom purposes are temporarily obstructed. Our displacement is a strategic loss at a critical time. The enemy scores a seeming victory, even if only for a season. For us, there is relief. We are out of that uncomfortable middle. And yet, it was to that middle that we were called. And that calling – to some middle – is relentless.

The Middle and Both Ends
Me – on the End

Much of prayer places us on "the end" of some blessing sought from God. It is never wrong to ask God to assist with personal needs, direction, protection, favor, healing – or any need. He is even concerned about the desires of our heart (Psalms 37:4). And yet, if we use prayer only as a means of acquisition from God, we will make a tragic mistake. *"Ye ask, and receive not, because ye ask amiss, that ye may consume it upon your lusts"* or desires (James 4:3).

James, the brother of Jesus says, *"You ask and do not receive."* Suddenly, heaven grows silent. God does not answer our prayers. What we request is not granted. It is *"because you ask amiss, that you may spend it on your pleasures"* (James 1:4). Whenever prayer becomes decidedly about us - God stops answering. James charges that in such moments, the spirit of the world has gripped our hearts, perhaps, without our even realizing we are caught in such a dynamic. He charges that our relationship with the world has made us "adulterers," and that such "friendship with the world" places us at "enmity with God?" Imperceptibly, we stepped across the line. We are now contributing, unwittingly, to the war against God. The remedy is humility. That is why Scripture says, *"God opposes the proud but gives grace to the humble"* (James 4:6, NIV).

Selfish praying entrenches us on the receiving end of all God's blessings. Underneath, buried in the heart of a genuine believer, is another prayerful cry, *"The Spirit who dwells in us yearns jealously?"* That is, God, by the Holy Spirit in us, has other designs and desires for us, better than we ourselves could acquire by selfish praying. Selfish praying isolates a blessing, seeing it in an exclusive way, as only for us. Spirit-led praying enlarges the blessing, seeing it as an inclusive way to bless others.

God – at the Beginning

God answers His people when we pray. Making requests of Him is a royal privilege. But, He does not want us to cement ourselves into the posture of always receiving for ourselves – of being "on the end" of all blessings.

The heart of all prayer is communion with God. That kind of prayer puts God first. It is prayer that honors God, as being on at the beginning, "the object" of our blessing, at the Head. It is prayer that is more about God, than me or you. It exalts God. It values Him. And value is the essence of worship. The very word, *worship* or *worth-ship,* is about value. Idolatry is ultimately about things, the things we worshipfully value. And life revolves around what we worshipfully value and, therefore, it should revolve around God. Sadly, He is only one among many, in a pantheon of things we value. The purest form of prayer is that which makes God the beginning and end, the highest of all things. He is first and foremost, central and supreme. We come to Him, not for what we can gain from Him, but because we have seen Him as the pearl of great price, the treasure in the field, the incomprehensible and incomparable God. The best prayer puts God at the beginning "on the receiving end" of our praise and adoration. Prayer at its heart is worship. It involves the deepest expressions of our love for the Creator and Redeemer.

If you will put God at "the beginning of prayer" and bless Him, He will put you on "the other end" and bless you. That is what happened to Abraham in Genesis 18. He entertained God, hosted Him, prepared a meal for Him, probably washed His feet – and in that encounter, Sarah's womb was opened and a 24 year promise that seemed stalled was fulfilled.[6] Sarah gave birth to a child, and Abraham gave birth to a nation. Communion with God is the basis of your and my right to offer petitions to God, to make requests of Him. *"If you abide in me, then you may ask"* (John 15:7), Jesus declared. It is the *relationship* that grants the *right* of prayer. No relationship – no right! We attempt to exploit the *right* of prayer and ignore the *relationship*. When the relationship deteriorates, the right is not easily exercised.

Isaiah declared to Israel, "*Your iniquities have separated you from your God; And your sins have hidden His face from you, So that He will not hear*" (Isaiah 59:2). John, writing in the New Testament offers the same counsel, *"Now we know that God does not hear sinners; but if anyone is a worshiper of God and does His will, He hears him"* (John 9:31). David declared, *"The righteous cry out, and the LORD hears"* (Psalm 34:17). Solomon echoed the same principle, *"The LORD is far from the wicked, but He hears the prayer of the righteous"* (Proverbs 15:29).

The nature of our relationship with God is one of righteousness. It is transformational. The essence of praying "in the name of Jesus" is the privilege of using the relationship that we now have with him to approach heaven in prayer. But to use the name of Jesus, and not feverishly honor the sanctity of that name by living in a way that brings honor to the divine and holy Father, is the essence of hypocrisy. The relationship grants the right and yet we dare not attempt to maintain the relationship to only retain the benefits. The relationship is not a mere means to something else. The relationship is the main thing.

Putting God on the receiving end of the blessing, God at the beginning of our attentions, at the head, and thereby making prayer less about acquisition and more about adoration, this is the first call of prayer. And then, God does bless. He breaks the barrenness. He whispers secrets, and He blesses our generations.

Then – to the Middle

Ultimately, God wants to move us to the middle. He wants to bless us, but more importantly, He wants to use us as a channel of blessing. He wants us in the uncomfortable, strategic, critical middle.

At times, others are called to the middle, as intercessors for us, and we are allowed to slip to the end. Beaten down by life, ambushed by some warfare experience, struggling to believe, and in the middle of a battle, others come to our aid and pray for us. Aaron and Hur did that for Moses (Exodus 17:12). They held his hands up as he sat on "the rock." Weak and unable to stand the pressure of the middle, other intercessors rushed to the middle to join the battle. And the tide against Amalek was turned. Who can understand such mysteries? The addition, and at times a multiplication of intercessors, secure the middle on the earth-side and win a victory.

The middle joins the beginning and the end. You can't be in the middle of a helping, transformative relationship, with a needy person on the earth-end, unless your communion with God in is secure. It is that primary relationship with Him that makes the helping relationship with the other, effectual. If you are in the middle holding onto one who has fallen off the cliff below you, the connection with the one above is vital, to both you and the one below. That is intercession. It doesn't work if you are not anchored and held securely by Christ.

Transformation – Not Merely Transaction

To achieve transformational outcomes, you have to have been transformed yourself. If you have never experienced the unconditional love of God, you cannot pass that on to another who desperately needs it.

Mature pray-ers get to the middle. They allow God to put them in the middle. Selfish pray-ers stay on the end, always asking for themselves. In the middle, my relationship with God allows me – to ask for others, particularly for those who have no covenant relationship, for those who need the bread of salvation. Again, the highest calling of prayer is communion with God, but its noblest use is intercession for the lost.

We often see prayer as a *transaction* with God. We make a request of Him and hope for an answer. We talk with God and wait for his reply. We give money and hope for a financial windfall. We exercise faith and believe for a breakthrough. We ask humbly for forgiveness and anticipate mercy. We request bread and look for it on the table. This is prayer's privilege, possible due to the goodness of God. But

> *The middle joins the beginning (God) and the end (others). You can't be in the middle of a helping, transformative relationship, with a needy person on the earth-end, unless your communion with God is secure. That primary relationship with Him, makes the helping relationship effectual.*

God is interested in more than a transactional relationship with us. He wants a transformational arrangement. He is willing to give us daily bread, but such grace should move us to share bread with others. He doesn't coach us to pray, give *me* my daily bread, but rather, give *us*. He assumes that we will pray – not from the end, but from the middle. That we will pray, not for ourselves alone, but with others in mind.

> *Focusing almost exclusively on the right of personal petition, while ignoring the responsibility of intercession (prayer for others) has left us with a narrow and less than holistic view of prayer, one that makes prayer almost solely about us.*

He, the giving God, wants to make of us, a giving people. He is willing to forgive us, but such shocking grace should so change us that we are then willing to forgive others. We want a single-dimensional legal transaction in which he commutes our sentence. He is not so much interested in having us "on the end" of grace, as he is in having us "in the middle" of grace. Forgiveness is to flow, not only *to* us, but *through* us.

We have developed a recipient mentality. God is the one to whom we go to receive - grace and blessings, forgiveness and mercy, direction and breakthrough, healing and deliverance, money for the rent and a pay raise for the future. With calculating faith, we reason that if we approach Him believing, with pure hearts and clean hands, on the basis of Scripture, then He will, He must hear us, and answer our prayer.

We make prayer about us. We make the priesthood of believers a personal and private thing. We have split ourselves off from others and sought private blessings. There is a time for using the privilege of personal petition. But, as with most things, God's ways are not our ways. Like the disciples, tired and worn out, he will often meet our needs not with us on the end of our own blessing, but in the middle of someone else's. Famished and weary, the disciples asked him to "send away" the hungry crowds (Mark 6:36). They wanted him alone to themselves. Instead, he took a young lad's lunch, and had them break and bless the meager meal, and divide it to thousands. When the disciple's stressful experience in the middle was over, there were twelve baskets full of fish and bread. Often, God's way of filling up our basket, is to put us in the middle of someone else's hunger.

We have fractured the theology of prayer. Focusing almost exclusively on the *right* of personal petition, while ignoring the *responsibility* of intercession (prayer for others) has left us with a narrow and less than holistic view of prayer, one that makes prayer about us. We have made Christianity *transactional*, when God intended for it to be *transformational*. He gives us bread, so that we become ourselves the givers of bread to others. He forgives us, as we act in forgiving ways, changed by the forgiveness of our own sins. He extends mercy, to make us merciful. He loves, but with the intention of making us loving agents of his own *agape*.

Transformation is His goal. Making us agents of His kingdom, from the strategic middle, is His objective.

---

1 Tolkien, *The Lord of the Rings: The Return of the King,* (New York: Ballentine Books, 1955), 12.
2 Ibid, 13.
3 Ibid, 14.
4 Ibid, 18.
5 Tolkien, *The Lord of the Rings: The Two Towers,* 275.
6 P. Douglas Small, *Entertaining God and Influencing Cities* (Kannapolis, NC: Alive Publications, 2008).

Discussion Guide

1. Discuss the power of being wrapped, clothed in the righteousness of Christ.
2. Have you ever considered the vulnerable place of Christ, in the middle, coming to the earth armed only with the power of innocent sinlessness, the original state of Adam, and having the charge to live a perfect life in order to redeem us and return to the Father in heaven? His was not a moon mission from which he might not have returned, but an earth mission.
3. We now stand in the middle, partnering with Jesus! What is our role in this 'middle'?
4. Talk about the tendency to pray 'on the end' of some blessing. To use prayer only as acquisition for some personal need.
5. James, the brother of Jesus, declared that unanswered prayers were sometimes a result of wrong motives and self-absorbed praying. Does that ever happen to you? What amount of our praying fits into this category? What does that say to the simple 'ask and believe,' to 'claiming what we want' in prayer?
6. What does it mean to be first put God 'on the end' of our prayer, to bless Him first?
7. Relationship grants the right of prayer - do you agree or disagree? What does that say about the need to work on the quality of our relationship?
8. What is the difference between prayer as a 'transaction' and prayer as a 'transforming' relationship?
9. Distinguish between the right of personal petition and the responsibility of intercession. Where do you think the average Christian is, in terms of percentage and time, in balancing these two? Why do Christians spend so little time in intercession?
10. What would it mean for you to be an 'agent of the kingdom' in some middle – at your job, in your neighborhood, at the next family reunion, at the local hospital, at your neighborhood school or fire station? What middle has God placed you in?

Gandalf to Pippen: *"There is no time to instruct you now in the history…though it might have been better, if you had learned something of it, when you were still birds-nesting and playing truant in the woods of the Shire."*[12]

Gandalf: *"If you have walked all these days with closed ears and mind asleep, wake up now!"*[13]

Then all the Captains of the West cried aloud, for their hearts were filled with new hope in the midst of darkness.

Gandalf: *"Stand, Men of the West! Stand and wait! This is the hour of doom!"* And even as he spoke the earth rocked beneath their feet…a vast soaring darkness sprang into the sky, flickering with fire. The earth groaned and quaked. The Towers of Teeth swayed, tottered, and fell down; the mighty rampart crumbled; the Black Gate was hurled in ruin; and from far way, now dim, now growing, now mounting to the clouds, there came a drumming rumble a roar, a long echoing roll of runious noise.[14]

CHAPTER FOUR
THE HISTORY OF THE RECURRING ABANDONMENT OF THE MIDDLE

Abraham and the Ancient Middle

When God called Abraham, He called him to the land we call Israel. He and his sons, Isaac and Jacob, were given the use of that land as a home. Abraham trekked the length and breadth of it. He decorated the landscape with altars. After arriving in the land, he built an altar at Shechem (Genesis 12:7). Then upon moving south, near Bethel, he again *"built an altar to the Lord and called on the name of the Lord"* (Genesis 12:8; Genesis 13:4). Thus, Yahweh, the name of the Lord and the land were joined; and they remain joined. When he and Lot separated, Abram moved to the region of Hebron and *"built an altar there to the Lord"* (Genesis 13:18). He later built one near Beersheba. And most significantly, God tested him, telling him to go to Moriah and offer Isaac as an offering. Upon their arrival, *"Abraham built an altar there"* (Genesis 22:9).

The land of Israel was loaned to Abraham and his children. In truth, it is not a land. It is a hallway. Located on the land-bridge that connects Europe, Asia and Africa, it was one of the most strategic pieces of real estate in ancient times. Every empire that rose needed to control that critical access point in the strategic middle of the earth. Read the Bible. All the ancient land empires are in its pages – Egypt, Assyria, Babylon, Media-Persia, the Greeks, and the Romans. All needed to control the land of Israel. God put His people in the middle of the earth. He chose the most strategic place in the ancient world for them to settle. He knew it would be a contested place. A bloody place. An uncomfortable and inconvenient place. But He knew, with Israel in such a place, the whole earth would know His name.

> *Priesthood was the destiny of Israel. They were to be a special treasure - a kingdom of priests. In earlier days, every godly and righteous man had been a priest... Now, all of Israel would serve as priests, deputized as representatives of God to nations around them.*

In the days of Jacob, the grandson of Abraham, the children of Israel retreated to Egypt to survive a famine. The banished favorite son of Jacob, Joseph, had become a cohort of Pharaoh. Hated by his brothers, he became their Savior. He thus became a type of the Messiah himself. Considered dead, he saved them from death. He protected them. He provided for them. They were the empowered older brothers who had excluded him. Now, he was the empowered and wounded brother, who included them. He forgave – and by his grace, they were saved. He was in the middle.

In time, he and his brothers would die. Their sons and daughters would no longer be treated so royally in Egypt. They would be considered outsiders and conscripted as slaves. Moses would be born. He would be sovereignly destined by God for the middle. Born a Hebrew, he would be raised as an Egyptian. Born a slave, he would be raised as a royal. Secretly, he would live in the middle, and then from the strategic middle, he would ultimately save his people.

Though a fugitive for a season, he would return to become the deliverer for Israel. He knew how to speak *to* Pharaoh, and how to speak *for* His people. That is the essence of priestly intercession. He knew the routes for the Exodus and the means by which they could endure the hardship of life in the wilderness. He knew the secrets of the Egyptian gods, but He would soon learn not only the secret name, *Yahweh*, of the God of Abraham, Isaac and Jacob; but also of his secret ways (Psa. 103:7). He was born for the middle. Multiple times, he would climb the mountain to meet with Yahweh. He was, like none before, and like none afterwards, until Jesus, the ultimate intercessor.

The Exodus and the Middle

Israel, following the leadership of Moses, was returning from Egypt to their Promised Land, the land of their fathers. God knew them, but they did not know Him. They had lived too long among the Egyptian gods. He brought them out of Egypt with a stunning and dashing miracle show. He triumphed over the gods of Egypt. And, a nation of slaves walked out as free men and women! But he did not take them directly into the land of promise. He parked them at the base of Sinai. He wanted them to know Him.

In the third month after the Exodus, God called to Moses:

> Moses went up to God, and the LORD called to him from the mountain, saying, Thus you shall say to the house of Jacob, and tell the children of Israel: You have seen what I did to the Egyptians, and how I bore you on eagles' wings and brought you to Myself (Exodus 19:3).

The wilderness was not a mere in-between place on the journey to *Canaan*. In truth, *Canaan* was not their destiny – *God* was their destiny. He did not want to give them a land. He wanted to give them the gift of Himself. It was not a land to which he wanted them attached – it was to Him that he wanted them joined. *"I bore you on eagles wings and <u>brought you to Myself</u>!"* Geography would not change Israel. Only a relationship with God would change them. The *right* to be in the land of promise depended upon that *relationship*. Only then could they be a credible and valuable representative people to the nations, while living in the middle of the ancient world.

> Now therefore, if you will indeed obey My voice and keep My covenant, then you shall be a special treasure to Me above all people; for all the earth is Mine. And you shall be to Me a kingdom of priests and a holy nation (Exodus 19:6).

Often overlooked, this was the destiny of Israel – not their poessession of a land; but God's possession of them. They were a special treasure to God – *a kingdom of priests*.[4] From the earliest days, every godly and righteous man had been his own priest, and had presented his own sacrifices before God – Abel (Genesis 4:3), Noah (Genesis 8:20), Abraham (12:7; 13:4), Isaac (26:25), Jacob (31:54), Job (Job 1:5) and Melchizedek (Genesis 14:18). The whole nation, every man among them, would now be a priest, in that same grand tradition. Not only in a personal sense or for his family, but he would be deputized as a representative of God to others and the whole nation would be a priestly people to the nations around them. In the middle of the earth, every member of every tribe would know God and tell the nations about him. No special class of priests – every Israelite a priest.

> *Moses came and called for the elders of the people, and laid before them all these words which the LORD commanded him. Then all the people answered together and said, "All that the LORD has spoken we will do." Moses brought back the words of the people to the LORD* (Exodus 19:7).

The deal was done. There was only one more step. God would now reveal Himself directly to the people. Moses would no longer be the exclusive go-between. Every man would know God. Everyone would be an intercessor.

> *And the LORD said to Moses, Behold, I come to you in the thick cloud, that the people may hear when I speak with you, and believe you forever* (Exodus 19:9).

Three days later, Israel had prepared themselves to meet Yahweh. Step into the story. Standing at the foot of the mountain, the whole nation is now to encounter Him. The sky is overcast. A gray heaven turns dark. A trumpet sounds. It is the signal to come near the mountain. Thunder can be heard in the distance. Flashes of lightning are observed. The cloud over the mountain grows more ominous, darker, and thicker. The sound of the trumpet intensifies. It is very loud, unnerving, and then the sound seems to be something beyond a mere natural trumpet blast. The whole atmosphere is eerie. Israel is having a paranormal spine-chilling experience. This is not a Sunday School picnic. *"All the people who were in the camp trembled"* (Exodus 19:16). People were physically shaking, quaking as a result of the power charged atmosphere. Even the plagues in Egypt did not have this effect on them.

Intercession – The Uncomfortable Strategic Middle

Mount Sinai was completely in smoke, because the LORD descended upon it in fire. Its smoke ascended like the smoke of a furnace, and the whole mountain quaked greatly (Exodus 19:19).

The ground is shaking, like it would as a result of a mild earthquake. And the sound of the trumpet, a blaring, ear-jabbing sound is escalating. No human could have made that sound. The *"blast of the trumpet sounded long and became louder and louder,"* Exodus 19:19.

> *Intimidated and fearful – they didn't want the intense faith encounter that God had designed. They wanted a cooler relationship. Not one that made them fear. They wanted someone between them and this disquieting Yahweh.*

Then Moses spoke and God answered him – by voice. Wow! What happens next is like something out of a science fiction novel. *"Then the LORD came down upon Mount Sinai"* and met with Moses. As His presence descended to the top of the mountain, the *"people witnessed the thunderings, the lightning flashes, the sound of the trumpet, and the mountain smoking"* (Exodus 20:19). It was all too much. *"When the people saw it, they trembled and stood afar off."* They backed away from the mountain. Instead of moving closer to God, they moved away from Him. They pleaded with Moses, *"You speak with us, and we will hear; but let not God speak with us, lest we die."* Moses attempted to calm their fears, *"Do not fear; for God has come to test you, and that His fear may be before you, so that you may not sin"* (Exodus 20:21).

The assurances were not enough. Lightning popped all around them. Thunder rolled. The earth shook. A typical thunderstorm releases the energy equivalent to twelve atomic bombs. Lightning travels at 186,000 miles per second, not from heaven to earth, but from earth to heaven. Negatively charged, ionized particles make an invisible chain, etching downward toward the surface of the earth in zigzagged, ragged patterns. The positive energy of the earth simultaneously leaps upward, with what scientists call "leaders." The moment one of those positively charged leaders connects with one of the chains of negative particles, spiraling downward, lightning races upward through the channel at the speed of light. The connection may be from a dew-laden blade of grass, the tip-top of a tree, the peak of a barn or a hair on a human head. When we see it, it is too late to duck. The fire at the core of a lightning bolt is three-to-five times hotter than the surface of the sun. No wonder *"the people stood afar off!"* The whole mountain appeared to be on fire, like a volcano. What a lightning show it must have been. Ground shaking thunder. The alarming and unsettling sound of the siren-like trumpet, piercing their ears. And yet, what they were seeing was not the power of God. It was only nature's reaction to His very real presence on top of the mountain. What an awesome God!

Intimidated and fearful, they refused the invitation to know Him. They didn't want the intense faith encounter that God had designed in order to instill a holy reverence in their souls. They wanted a milder religion. They wanted to know God – but only indirectly. They wanted to hear from Him, but through someone else. They wanted a cooler and more distant relationship – not such a close and terrorizing one. Not one that made them fear. Not one that put a reverence in their hearts. Not one that seemed strange and unearthly. They wanted someone in the middle, someone between them and this disquieting Yahweh. He, conversely, wanted them in the middle. He wanted the whole nation to know Him, every Israelite, in order that they might be His personal representatives, a kingdom of priests.

Israel, the nation in the middle of the earth, called to minister to all the nations of the earth – that was His plan. Every son of Abraham would be a priest, capable of ministering to any man or woman on the earth and introducing them to Yahweh and His ways. Their redemptive story would be the model for the nations. Their good and gracious God was the God of the whole earth. *"The earth is mine,"* He had told them. He wanted to give them a critical slice of it, as custodians, if they would represent Him. But they said, *"No!"* Unbelievable. Stunning. What a setback for Israel. What a tragedy for the nations – a vacant center would continue in the middle of the nations.

"Moses drew near the thick darkness where God was," and Israel backed away. In the end, Aaron and his sons would become a layer of priests between God and the people. As a special class of priests, they would be in the middle, between Yahweh and Israel. But for the nations, the middle would be effectively vacant. Israel had rejected its role as a priest-nation. It would be the prescription for their defection from the faith. You backslide from the end. After Solomon's death, the nation would divide. Israel, comprised of the ten northern tribes, would be carried to Assyria, never to return. Judah, the remaining tribe, would eventually be carried to Babylon.

The middle would again be completely deserted.

The Returning Captives from Babylon and the Middle

Isaiah declared that a tenth would return from captivity (Isaiah 6:13). And indeed they did. In B.C. 605, Babylon's armies had first come to Jerusalem. In B.C. 586, they destroyed the city completely, including the great and grand temple of Solomon.

The History of the Recurring Abandonment of the Middle

The city would be inhabited by foxes for decades. It would lie completely in ruins. The light to the nations, though never the beacon God had intended, had now gone out completely. Then, under the Persians, the Emperor Cyrus would allow the first of the refugees to return. Coming back in B.C. 535, they would live among the ruins created by the Babylonian captivity. They would exist in a survival mode. To them and for them, Isaiah set forth a dramatic and startling restoration plan.

> *Here it was again, the call to be a "servant nation!" All of them, every person, would bear an anointing. All would share the good news. All would heal the brokenhearted – a nation of healers. All would liberate captives.*

> *The Spirit of the Lord God is upon me, Because the Lord has anointed me to preach good tidings to the poor; He has sent me to heal the brokenhearted, to proclaim liberty to the captives, And the opening of the prison to those who are bound; to proclaim the acceptable year of the Lord, and the day of vengeance of our God; to comfort all who mourn, to console those who mourn in Zion, to give them beauty for ashes, the oil of joy for mourning, the garment of praise for the spirit of heaviness; that they may be called trees of righteousness, the planting of the Lord, that He may be glorified* (Isaiah 61:1-3).

Here it was again, the call to be a "servant nation!" All of them, every person, would bear an anointing. All would share the good news. All would heal the brokenhearted – a nation of healers. All would liberate captives and unshackle the bound. Every year would be a year of Jubilee, the year that Israel was never willing to experience in the pre-exilic period. Tears would be replaced with comfort. Mourning over losses, would be ended by the divine gift of new hope. Ashes would be replaced by holy turbans of beauty, crowns of glory. Depression would be broken, and joy would break forth. Israel would be planted in the land because every man had a relationship with God. They would be like a garden for the nations – trees of righteousness, an Eden-like paradise in the middle of the earth. It would be a new day. *"You shall be named the priests of the Lord... (Men) shall call you the servants of our God"* (Isaiah 61:6).

They were back, in a sense, at Sinai. There, Israel had rejected the priesthood as a nation. They had chosen the end and not the middle. In the vacant middle, they had inserted a priesthood for the nation. As a result, they apostacized. Pluralism, with what must have seemed at first benign elements of paganism, had claimed all twelve tribes, first exiled to Assyria, and then to Babylon. Now, a remnant was back wondering how to proceed.

Isaiah offered the solution. In the reorganization of national spiritual life, there should be no special class of priests. Instead, the whole nation should be a kingdom of priests. Everyone must know God. Everyone was to be anointed. Everyone was called to proclaim the good news. Everyone was to be an instrument of healing. Everyone would bind up broken hearts and offer deliverance. They were back on track!

But it didn't happen that way. Again, they rejected the middle. Instead, Judah rebuilt the temple, but not for the nations, only for themselves. And they installed a priest-hood more restrictive than before. They knew that they had fallen as a nation by not keeping the law, by first accommodating to the gods of the Gentiles, allowing them a place in the culture. Then, by open idolatry, by worshipping those idols. Now they would go to the other extreme. They would not only reject foreign idols, they would essentially reject foreigners. They would become fiercely closed. Legalism would triumph. They would not fall again by the mistake of not keeping the law. They would go beyond and above the law. And they did. Jesus would say that they had shut up the kingdom (Matthew 23:13-14). They heard only a part of Sinai's offer. And they rejected the liberating and centering vision and mission offered through Isaiah.

Jesus and the Middle Reclaimed

When Jesus came, Israel had so misunderstood the purpose of the law that it had become a massive burden to the common man, an obstruction to righteous living, rather than a recipe for godly and viable principles for daily life (Matthew 23:4). A lifestyle of holiness and righteousness intended to distinctively mark them for the purpose of witnessing to the nations, and to preserve them had become convoluted by their self-righteousness, pride, and sectarianism. The law, meant to protect them, had become an excuse for not helping others (v. 4). It had produced a condition of arrogance, without love and compassion (Matthew 23:5-12). Israel was keeping the law, but they were no closer to their destiny than at any time before.

Rather than posturing with openness, they had shut up the kingdom to themselves (Matthew 23:13). Rather than sharing the good news, they saw themselves as exclusive custodians of a private blessing. They engaged in social oppression while acting godly and spiritual in public (Matthew 23:14). Clean by the standards of the law, they had a scandalous mess in their hearts (Matthew 23:25). Tragically, they were so blind they could not see their own error, even when it was pointed out (Matthew 23:26). They were spiritually dead. Superficially lawful, they were profoundly lawless – a deadly and deceitful combination (Matthew 23:28). They rationalized history,

> *If we had lived in the days of our fathers, we would not have been partakers with them in the blood of the prophets* (Matthew 23:30).

They were blind. In fact, they would not only not recognize the ultimate prophet, they would be complicit in crucifying the Son of God and become witnesses against themselves (Matthew 23:31).

> O Jerusalem, Jerusalem, the one who kills the prophets and stones those who are sent to her! How often I wanted to gather your children together, as a hen gathers her chicks under her wings, but you were not willing! See! Your house is left to you desolate; for I say to you, you shall see Me no more till you say, 'Blessed is He who comes in the name of the LORD!' (Matthew 27:37).

> GANDALF: Deep in, but not at the bottom, you have forgotten Saruman. He began to take an interest in the Shire before Mordor did.
>
> MERRY TO GANDALF: Well, we've got you with us.
>
> GANDALF: I am with you at the present, but soon I shall not be. I am not coming to the Shire. You must settle its affairs yourselves; that is what you have been trained for. Do you not yet understand? My time is over; it is no longer my task to set things to rights...you are grown up now.[5]

The middle was left vacant, except for the priestly ministry to the nation itself, and the people remained on the comfortable end. For the nations, the earth itself, the middle was empty, without a representative. Access to Yahweh through Israel was shut off to the nations.

Jesus walked into the synagogue and picked up the scroll. He unwound it to Isaiah, and he read:

> The Spirit of the LORD is upon Me, because He has anointed Me to preach the gospel to the poor; He has sent Me to heal the brokenhearted, to proclaim liberty to the captives, and recovery of sight to the blind, to set at liberty those who are oppressed; to proclaim the acceptable year of the LORD (Luke 4:18-19).

He would call twelve disciples and give them authority to preach the gospel. *"And when He had called His twelve disciples to Him, He gave them power over unclean spirits, to cast them out, and to heal all kinds of sickness and all kinds of disease"* (Matthew 10:1). These men were not from the priestly caste. They were common men. Jesus had called the nation back to Exodus 19 and Isaiah 61. He envisioned a kingdom of ordinary believers, functioning as priests.

> *These twelve Jesus sent out and commanded them, saying... As you go, preach, saying, 'The kingdom of heaven is at hand.' Heal the sick, cleanse the lepers, raise the dead, cast out demons. Freely you have received, freely give* (Matthew 10:5-8).

Their mission was to shake up whole cities. It was a confrontational mission. They were sheep in the midst of wolves (v. 17). They would be delivered up to councils and beaten up in synagogues (v. 18). They would stand before governors and kings. Eventually, they would testify not only to Israel, but to the nations (v. 19).

At another time, *"He appointed seventy others also, and sent them two by two before His face into every city and place where He Himself was about to go"* (Luke 10:1). *"Heal the sick there,"* he told them, and say to them, *"The kingdom of God has come near to you."*

Isaiah ended his words about the anointing with this note.

> *As a bride adorns herself with her jewels...as the earth brings forth its bud, as the garden causes the things that are sown in it to spring forth, so the Lord GOD will cause righteousness and praise to spring forth before all the nations* (Isaiah 61:11).

They were to be like a beautiful bride – adorned and ready for a wedding. Their spiritual renewal was to be so profound, that it affected the earth itself – creating a budding earth, in a new season of springtime, with seeds coming to life and new plants breaking forth. Praise was to spring forth among the nations! What does it mean?

God's intentions were to begin in the middle – and move outward, missionally. To start with one people, Israel – and through them reach all peoples. That required a whole nation, a spiritually healthy nation, and one in an intimate relationship with Him, not one with a special class of exclusive priests. The experiment had failed. So, God Himself, in Christ, came to the middle. And after his ascension and enthronement, with the coming of the Spirit, he called his bride-partner, the Church, adorned with holiness and anointed with the fragrant oil of the Spirit, to join Him in the middle.

Positioning a New People in the Middle

For three-and-a-half years, Jesus ministered, much of that time, in the context of the twelve disciples. He taught and trained them from the middle. He mentored. He discipled them. When the smoke had cleared and he had ascended, the twelve had become 120. On the Day of Pentecost, they were all gathered in the Upper Room at his request, obediently waiting. When the Day of Pentecost had fully come, there was a rumble. And then fire. There was a sound – like wind, like a storm, like a roar. It was Sinai all over again. This time, the law would not be written on tablets of stone, but on tender hearts. This time there would be no backing away from the fiery mountain. This group would fellowship with the fire. The whole room appeared to be in flames. Then the fire de-

> *This time, there would be no backing away from the fiery mountain. This group would fellowship with the fire. They broke the language barrier. The nations heard.*

scended, touching each of them. Ecstasy consumed them. Native tongues could no longer express what they now felt and understood. They broke the language barrier. The nations heard. Flooding onto the streets, they took their joy to the city. The Feast of Pentecost insured that *"devout men, from every nation under heaven"* (Acts 2:5) were gathered in the streets of the city. And they were about to have a divine encounter. It is what God had longed for. A people, though a small group, now knew Him directly. They were in the middle. Potential representatives to the nations were about to be blessed and introduced to the resurrected Christ.

> *And when this sound occurred, the multitude came together, and were confused, because everyone heard them speak in his own language. Then they were all amazed and marveled, saying to one another, "Look, are not all these who speak Galileans? And how is it that we hear, each in our own language in which we were born? Parthians and Medes and Elamites, those dwelling in Mesopotamia, Judea and Cappadocia, Pontus and Asia, Phrygia and Pamphylia, Egypt and the parts of Libya adjoining Cyrene, visitors from Rome, both Jews and proselytes, Cretans and Arabs – we hear them speaking in our own tongues the wonderful works of God (Acts 2:6-11).*

The nations heard that day! And the New Testament church was off and running – operating from the critical, strategic, uncomfortable and sometimes bloody middle. They would see the death of James and the martyrdom of Stephen, the multiple imprisonment of disciples and apostles. They would experience persecution. They would be dragged into court, illegally charged, and treated shamefully. They would be beaten and imprisoned in stocks. But in the end, the redeemed lambs would defeat the roaring lion, Satan. They would turn the world upside down. City after city would come under the influence of the rag-tag band of common, but extraordinary men and women. Mortals performed miracles. Simple men preached profound truth.

Constantine would become the first Christian Emperor (A.D. 312). Emperor Theodosius would make Christianity the faith of the empire (A.D. 380). The pagans had lost! The Christians had won. The cross was in; the idols were out.

> *Luther's notion of priesthood was not so much that I could pray - as a priest, for myself and myself alone, but rather that we could and would all pray for one another.*

It was the most wonderful and terrible thing that had happened since the crucifixion and the resurrection. The political declaration became the opportunity for non-Christians to flood into the church. Before, men had paid a price to identify with Christ. Before, they needed to know God. Before, they had to make a radical decision for discipleship. Before, it was unpopular. Now, the emperor was a believer. Christianity was fashionable. It was the cultural norm. It was both an end and a beginning; a triumph and a tragedy.

The Drift from the Middle to the End

Suddenly and unthinkably, the church began to do what Israel had done. It drifted from the middle, and back to the end. Now fashionable, the church filled up with pagans who professed faith. But they did not climb the smoking, fiery mountain. The church no longer had a membership who feared God because they had fellowshipped with the fire. These people had not witnessed any thunder. They had heard no mighty rushing wind. They did not know the Lord. They only knew someone who did. They were on the end, not in the middle.

It would take centuries, just as it did with Israel, for the effects of living on the end to have its final result. Like Israel, the Church fell into apostasy. The ministry evolved into an exclusive priest-hood for the common people. Soon, it along occupied the middle, allowing the people to remain on the end. The Bible was taken from them and from their hearts. The altar, really the table of the Lord, was removed from the people. A veil came to separate the gathered congregation and the platform, where the priests prayed, not the people. It was a reversion to a form of Old Testament tabernacle and temple worship. Legalism replaced life. The song of the people was gone. Sin abounded. Holiness of heart perished. Corruption became the norm. Praying was done through a man, not to and through the resurrected Christ, not in the name of Jesus by the enabling power of the Holy Spirit. At first, they prayed through a mortal, priestly, man – then eventually, it would be through deceased men and women in heaven – the saints. The central and exclusive role of Jesus, as the only way to God, the Father, was compromised by prayers offered through priests, through Mary and the saints. Forgiveness came through the church, not through the shed blood of his sacrifice alone, based on grace, accessed by heartfelt repentance. The middle was highjacked by pseudo agents of a false grace, all offering alternative access points to God. The middle to which the whole church had been called was now filled with agents who kept ordinary men and women at a distance from the Divine. Indulgences and theological corruption encouraged an already sinful people.

The Reformation – A Call back to the Middle

On October 31, 1517, a monk by the name of Martin Luther posted ninety-five theses on the doors of the Castle Church in Wittenberg, Germany. The action was the customary way of advertising an event on a university campus. Church doors often functioned like bulletin boards. Evidence suggests, however, that Luther was not passive, that this was not a business-as-usual act, that he also mailed copies of the theses to the Archbishop of Mainz, sent them to the Pope, to his friends and other universities. He was looking for a fight! He was starting a revolution.

On that day in October, Luther approached church authorities with his pressing call for reform. He presented them with his theses, and he requested that they stop the activities of the indulgence preachers. The bishops did not respond. So Luther circulated his theses publicly. "The Ninety-five Theses" spread quickly. They were printed in Nuremberg, Leipzig, and Basel. Suddenly, they were circulating throughout Germany and beyond its borders.

The reformation was on! Principal among the cornerstone elements was the concept of the priesthood of all believers. God was calling the Church back to the middle. The Church would have pastors, but the people would not have priests. Every believer would be a priest, with direct access to heaven itself, to God as Father, through Christ his Son. And yet, every believer would also be a willing intercessor, to and for others, particularly to and for the lost. Yet, no intercessor would claim the right to stand between any sincere believer and God.

The *Ninety-Five Theses* met with enormous popularity in a very short period of time. Luther's ideas resonated with people regardless of class, status or wealth. Pope Leo X would issue a rebuttal to Luther. But his word would not end the debate. Luther's theses became a kind of declaration of independence in the churches of Northern Europe. Around the idea rallied enormous social changes. By 1522, much of Wittenberg had begun celebrating Lutheran services instead of Roman Catholic services. The people were now moving back to the middle. They were talking to God again – directly.

The table of the Lord was given back to the people. The song was restored to the people. The Scripture was translated into the common tongue. The mysterious Latin mass was replaced by worship in their common language. Prayer again became the believer's privilege. And yet, Luther's notion of priesthood was not so much that I could pray – from the end, for myself and myself alone, but rather that we could and would all pray for one another – from the middle. It was not so much that men could now or were being encouraged to bypass all others, with a private and individual relationship with God that excluded others. It was, rather, that men could now pray in a way that included all others; indeed, that embraced the world.

Tragically, the doctrine of the priesthood all believers has been interpreted as a private and personal relationship with God, as something exclusive and closed. It has allowed for a privatized Christianity to emerge. No such faith exists in the pages of the Bible. You and I can pray to God without anyone but Christ between us. And yet, that is not the essence of the idea of the priesthood of believers. Luther meant that ordinary men and women could and should pray for other men and women, everywhere. I could and should be a priest for you, and you for me. It was a call to the middle. It was a call to offer the gift of our the faith to the world, through prayer. It was a call to introduce all to God through prayer. And to connect God to all, through intercessory prayer.

The Protestant Drift

The Protestant church would not have priests, it would have pastors. And yet, far too quickly, the pastoral craft would behave similar to its predecessor, the priestly caste. Pastors, though called to act in priestly ways, and to model the middle, were never meant to be our priests. Sadly, the church has treated pastors like priests. And pastors have sometimes held the middle ground as exclusively belonging to them. They have chosen to do the praying – for the church, the community, the sick and the lost. And the church has been the weaker and less spiritual as a result.

The Protestant Reformation placed the Bible in the hands of the people. It called people to a level of prayer never known in the generations of the Middle Ages before them. It sparked renewal and awakening. It kindled movements of prayer. It generated revival movements, evangelism and mission endeavors. Not all the church was praying, but some were. Movements of regenerative grace were followed by movements of sanctification. Pastors were soon joined by evangelists. Churches resistant to change, found themselves set aside, as Wesley and Whitefield did something that had not happened since the Church had gone indoors in the days of Constantine, virtually since the days of Christ - they preached in open fields and on hill-sides to the masses. They broke bread to thousands, serving communion, to people from whole cities, and vast regions.

Out of these experiences, came the camp-meeting movements. Missionaries arose, and went to the far corners of the world, to those who had never heard the gospel, in order to proclaim the good news. God was up to something!

Sadly, it would not be enough. Soon, Protestant clergy would again occupy the middle for a Protestant laity who preferred the comfortable and non-challenging end. Pastors were soon standing in the same relational space where Roman priests had previously stood, and the laity was a long way from climbing the mountain and meeting God.

The drift to the end is the essence of apostasy. The call to the middle is relentless. God will one day have a people in the critical, strategic middle.

The History of the Recurring Abandonment of the Middle

1. Tolkien, *The Lord of the Rings: The Return of the King*, 11.
2. Ibid.
3. Ibid, 243.
4. The term priest comes from the Old English or Anglo Saxon word *prest*, or *preost*, or *pre['o]st*. It is also related to the French or Latin term presbyter, and the Greek term elder, older, or old man. The first syllable of which is probably akin to Latin *pristinus*, related to Pristine, Presbyter. In the New Testament, the word most often translated priest is the Greek *hierus*, or *hiereus* – holy! The Latin equivalent of that term is *sacerdos*, related to our English world sacred. In Hebrew, the most common term is *kohen*, from an unknown derivative (*ko-hane'*). A related word in Hebrew is *kahan* (*kaw-han'*), which means "to act as a priest." This is a denominative verb from *kohen*, with an etymology meaning "to deck" or to put on specific and perhaps, elaborate and distinctive garments. A priest not only acts in a role, but his wardrobe reflects that role. In the New Testament, the use of the term holy and sacred, may provide the really important connection. To be a priest, to act as a priest, we must put on holiness. Even in the Old Testament, the garments of the priest are holy. Related to the term of the priest is a Latin term often used for the high priest of the church, or in the case of the Roman Church, the Pope. The term is *maximus pontifex*. The term *maximus* is great. The term *pontifex* or *pontiff* is a bridge builder. It comes from *pont*, a stem of *pons* "bridge" with *fex*, *ficis*, a root of *facere*, to "make." If so, the word originally meant "bridge-maker," or "path-maker." The term is not exclusively Christian. It was used in a broader way – "bridge-building has always been regarded as a pious work of divine inspiration." And it was used as a metaphor for bridging the earthly world and to the realm of the gods. (See http://www.etymonline.com/index.php?search=pontifex&searchmode=none)
5. Tolkien, *The Lord of the Rings: The Return of the King*, 298.

Discussion Guide

1. What is the implication of the geography of the Bible, of Israel being in the middle? What implication does that have for the church? Why are we not 'in the middle?' Why does it feel like the church is on a side street, culturally unengaged?

2. God wanted Israel, the whole nation, to be a 'kingdom of priests'. Does he want the same for the church?

3. What is difference between a pastor and laity as believer-priests? What do we mean when we speak of the priesthood of all believers?

4. Do we only mean that we can pray directly to the Father, through the Son, by the enabling of the Spirit, according to the Scripture? Or is more involved? I the priesthood of believers merely a private matter?

5. God declared to Israel, that His desire was to "bring them to Himself" – and that relationship would qualify them to be his representatives. Talk about how the quality of our personal relationship with God defines our caring relationship with others.

6. Israel did not want to be 'in the middle.' They chose the end – and both the northern and southern tribes would backslide. Do you think you backslide more easily from 'the comfortable end?' If so, why?

7. Israel, as a nation was to experience 'the anointing!' That anointing would empower them to make a difference among the poor, the brokenhearted, the captives and the bound. Do you think we see the anointing as empowering us to reach the same conditions in humans around us?

8. Israel was called to be a servant nation. Is the church called to be a servant people as well? Who does your church serve - in the city, or some foreign mission field? Or we merely serve one another? Who should we serve? If we are called to be a servant-people, and we are not, can we really call ourselves a legitimate church?

9. Talk about the similarities and differences between Sinai and Pentecost. How were the two encounters alike? How were the outcomes different?

10. How could the Church back away from the middle – and into the Dark Ages? What would it take to reform today's church, and move it back to the middle?

Small men may do the greater deeds.[1]

ARAGORN: *"The worst is now over. Stay and be comforted!"* He laid two leaves on his hands and breathed on them… living freshness filled the room, as if the air itself awoke and tingles, sparkling with joy. At once hearts were lightened. The fragrance was like a memory of dewy mornings of unshadowed sun in some land of which the fair world in Spring is itself by a fleeting memory. *"Farewell then for a while. I must go to others who need me!"*

IORETH: *"King! The hands of a healer."* And soon the word had gone out from the House that the king was indeed come among them, and after war he brought healing; and the news ran through the City.[2]

GIMLI: *"There are countless things still to see in Middle-earth, and great works to do. But if all the fair folk take to the Havens, it will be a duller world for those who are doomed to stay."*

MERRY: *"Dull and dreary indeed."* [3]

CHAPTER FIVE
THE FINAL CALL TO THE MIDDLE

A century ago, a new phenomenon spontaneously erupted around the world. In a cosmopolitan city like Los Angeles and a remote mountain community called Camp Creek, NC, in little hamlets and far-flung places on the globe, Azusa Street experiences in the Spirit began to initiate ordinary people into a supernatural anointing. Signs and wonders abounded. Like the Jerusalem company of 120, rightly accused of being uneducated and common, simple folks again were fellowshipping with the fire. God was calling his church back to the middle.

Out of the Pentecostal movement came a global awakening, still not given its rightful place by stuffy church historians. It was simultaneously a culturally impacting movement and a major church-shift. Common laymen became preachers. Ordinary men and women became intercessors whose mysterious prayer journeys were evidenced by calloused knees and hostile hearts who became friends and then believers, by closed cities who mysteriously embraced the message they first ferociously fought. A professional preacher was not necessary. Anyone could pray the prayer of faith for people around them who were in need and do it anywhere. Storefronts became churches. Brush arbors became platforms for proclamation. Street corners became chapels. The fire blazed around the globe. By the time of the half-century, leaders such as Henry P. Van Dusen of Union Theological Seminary were calling it "the third force in Christendom!"[4]

Azusa Street – the Middle of the World

In the beginning, the meetings on Azusa Street ran seven days a week, almost around the clock. In 1922, William J. Seymour, the African-American who led the great revival would die, but the services were still continuing. In the early days, one characteristic of the meeting was joy manifest in what they called the "heavenly chorus."[5] Visitors would report, "I found myself suddenly joining the rest who had received this supernatural 'gift.' It was a spontaneous manifestation and rapture no earthly tongue can describe... wonderfully pure and powerful. We feared to try to reproduce it..."[6] No one had preached it. No one encouraged it. The Lord bestowed it. The effect was extraordinary. It produced a heavenly atmosphere as though the angels themselves were joining humans. Even wicked men had difficulty offering ridicule. The music was a pure and spontaneous blend of voices, there were no musical instruments. There was no place for them and no need for them. The singing was superb. Hymnals were not used. Songs were offered from memory, quickened by the Spirit.

Ordinary People – Fellowshipping with Fire

Ordinary people experiencing the powerful reality of the presence of God – that was Azusa Street. Prideful displays and fleshly aberrations, along with false prophesies and people seeking attention, were shut down by the Spirit. "The crow cannot imitate the dove," they would say. Common people were endowed with uncommon discernment.[7]

Seymour was the leader, but he was not a dominant or even a dynamic leader.[8] His head was bowed most of the time, sometimes hidden in the makeshift pulpit comprised of two crates stacked one on top of the other. He led by example. He led quietly. There was, in fact, more of a "brotherhood" mentality that reigned, a display of humility among equals. There was no hierarchy. There was no one person directing the experience for all others. There was no priest class or craft. All accessed the glorious presence of God. The Lord Himself was leading the prayer gatherings. That a one-eyed, illiterate, black-man would be chosen by God to lead a city-shaking revival was too much for some. What kind of leader stays on his knees much of the time with his face hidden in prayer? Maybe just the kind that God is looking for again!

> *Everyone sought to honor and obey God. It became a wonderfully fearful thing to hinder or grieve the Spirit. The whole place was soaked in prayer. It was a prayer meeting - the Church in session with God. God was in His holy temple. Man needed to be silent. Sieges of silence were not uncommon.*

Hungry Humble Hearts

Seeking souls could be found under the influence of the power of the Holy Spirit at almost any hour, night and day. At the height of the movement, Azusa Street was never closed and rarely empty. People came, not to a service, but to meet God. He was always there. The old building was no show-place. It was only 40 feet by 60 feet. Yet, up to 1500 people would crowd in. Today, the building might be rated to seat no more than 250 or so. Those who could not get in stood peering in at the windows. The walls were charred and black. The building was ugly. It had low rafters providing only an eight-foot ceiling and bare floors. It had been a foundry, a livery stable, and then a warehouse. It was still a warehouse – a work place where God broke strong men and women, and then put them back together again for His glory. It was a humble place that elicited humility. Pride and self-assertion, self-importance and self-esteem, could not survive there.[10]

No subjects or sermons were announced ahead of time. No special speakers were featured. No one knew what would happen, what God would do. Everything was spontaneous. People came, not

> *Surely you don't disbelieve the prophecies, because you had a hand in bringing them about yourself? You don't really suppose, do you, that all your adventures and escapes were managed by mere luck, just for your sole benefit? You are a very fine person, Mr. Baggins, and I am very fond of you; but you are only quite a little fellow in a wide world after all.*[9]

to hear from man, but to hear from God – through whoever might speak. There was no "respect of persons." The ground in the middle is level.[11]

A Spirit of Unity

The rich and poor came. The educated and the ignorant came. All were equal. All had to die. Only God was glorified. The meetings often started spontaneously with no formal beginning. People came hungry. Real testimonies burst forth out of fresh heart-experiences. A dozen people would be on their feet at any one time, trembling under the power of God. Still, order prevailed out of reverence for God. In honor, each "preferred one another."[12] Anyone could be divinely used of the Lord. This was, in fact, the prayer of the whole group, that all might be used of God. No one true saint wished attention. The great joy was not from sharing, but from the fact that God was working in and through all. Common people were being used. Ordinary laymen were fellowshipping with fire.

At times, someone would rise to speak, and suddenly the Spirit would fall upon the congregation. God himself would give the altar call. Men would fall all over the house, like the slain in battle. The scene resembled a forest of fallen trees. They would rush for the altar as one, to seek God. One observer said, "I never saw an altar call given by a man. God would call them."[13]

No Flesh Glorified – Reverence for God!

Everyone sought to honor and obey God. It became a wonderfully fearful thing to hinder or grieve the Spirit. The whole place was soaked in prayer. It was a prayer meeting – the Church in session with God. God was in His holy temple. Man needed to be silent. Sieges of silence were not uncommon. The Upper Room, a dedicated room on the second floor, was set aside for vigilant prayer and seekers, but the rule was, "No talking above a whisper."[14]

Wave after wave of revival swept the people in that building. The people would move from tears to triumph. They would weep over sin one minute and praise God for pardon the next. Testimonies decorated the meetings. People told of miraculous healings, of divine provision for those in poverty. After the services were over, folks stood around. Some continued praying. Others went to the second-floor seeking-room. No one wanted to leave. Everyone was fearful of missing something. They were in the presence of God. Some claim to have seen a cloud of glory over the building by night. The presence of God was said to have been so heavy, that people reported being knocked to the ground, blocks from the mission.

When self-promoting preachers attempted to assert their opinions and gain exposure in the meeting, inordinate things would occur. Some would find their breath taken from them. Some would become confused and unable to complete sentences. The people would sense an arrogant attitude and they would pray. At times, presumptuous men would simply collapse in mid-speech. In most cases, they could not go on for long. No one cut them off. They were stopped by the Spirit, some carried out like dead men.

Others were transformed into a state of humility. And in childlike fashion, they cried out to God in a confession of personal weakness and need, and God filled them with the Holy Spirit. With a crowded middle, filled with common people who were experiencing God first-hand, preachers often felt threatened and ignored. They died the hardest.

Soon after the revival broke, the crowds were both multi-racial and multi-national. Integration prevailed in a city that had been known for racism. There was no racial prejudice in the services.

African-Americans, Caucasian Americans, Chinese and Jews all attended the services. Frank Bartleman, an Azusa Street historian would exclaim, "The color line is washed away in the blood!"[15] And all by the work of the Spirit. The hunger for God overcame the hatred between races. Some called Azusa Street a "disgraceful intermingling of the races." God might have called it unity. In fact, "Love, faith, unity" were the watch words.[16]

Transformed Lives

Those who came to Azusa Street with racial issues often testified to a transformation. Many southern Caucasian-Americans were disturbed by the interracial worship. When G. B. Cashwell arrived at Azusa Street and learned that Seymour was black, he was troubled. Cashwell, a southern preacher, was deeply prejudiced against African-Americans. He returned to his hotel room and there he experienced a "crucifixion." That day he "died" to "his racial prejudice." The next night, he humbled himself and asked Seymour, and other African-American men, to lay hands on him

> *This call to the middle, at the beginning of the 20th century, launched the greatest expansion in global missions ever! Seventy-percent of all those who have come to Christ since A.D. 100, have come since Azusa Street. Pentecostal empowerment and witness go hand-in-hand. The fullness of the Spirit is not an addition to salvation, not an experiential trinket. It is an anointing to participate in the priestly ministry of Jesus.*

and pray that he be filled with the Holy Ghost. They did. He was. And Cashwell became one of the most extraordinary evangelists of the outpouring.[17]

The *Apostolic Faith* newspaper printed in September, 1906, described the first meetings like this.

> The meetings began about ten o'clock in the morning and can hardly stop before ten or twelve at night, and sometimes two or three in the morning, because so many are seeking, and some are slain under the power of God. People are seeking three times at the altar. We cannot tell how many people have been saved, and baptized with the Holy Ghost, and healed of all manner of sicknesses. Many are speaking in new tongues and some are going on their way to the foreign fields with the gift of the language. A drunkard got under conviction in a street meeting and raised his hands to be prayed for. They prayed for the devil of drink to be cast out, and the appetite was gone. He came to the meeting and was saved, sanctified and baptized with the Holy Ghost, and in three days from the time he was drunk he was speaking in a new tongue and praising God for Pentecost. He hardly knows himself.

Into All the World

Soon, people from all over the world were making a trip to Azusa Street. The list of these people is like a Who's Who of early Pentecostal leaders. Florence Crawford who took the message to the Northwest. William H. Durham who touched the Mid-Western United States. Elder Sturdevant, an African-American, who founded the first Pentecostal church in New York City. G. B. Cashwell from North Carolina who touched the Pentecostal Holiness church, the Church of God and the Church of God of Prophecy, as well as the Pentecostal Free-Will Baptists. Glenn A. Cook who touched Indiana. C. H. Mason of the Church of God in Christ fame from Tennessee. Samuel Saell from Arizona and Rachael Sizelove from Missouri. R. E. McAlister took the message to Ottawa, Canada. T. B. Barratt, a Norwegian Methodist, took the message to Sweden, Norway, Denmark, Germany, France and England. Many of these leaders founded Pentecostal denominations.[18]

Breaking the Language Barrier

The experiences were mind bending. Once, a skeptical Jewish man attended the mission. His goal was to gather first-hand evidence against speaking in tongues that he could then use it in lectures against Christianity. Entering a staircase in the mission, a young woman stopped and pointed at him. She spoke in perfect Hebrew, his native language. She called his first name, his last name, and then proceeded to tell him what he was doing in Los Angeles. If that was not enough, she gave him a record of his sins. Still skeptical, he asked her where she had learned Hebrew. She confessed that she didn't know Hebrew. She was simply speaking by the Spirit. Convicted, he fell to his knees and repented on the spot.[19]

One historian noted, "People would come into the meeting and they'd hear their language – Russian and Armenian and various languages – and they would hear the Gospel being preached. And they would come running to the altar, asking, 'How do you know my language?' and give their hearts to the Lord."[20]

On June 16, 1906, a short time after the revival started, the first white pastor was filled with the Spirit. He had directed his congregation to attend services at the Azusa Street mission, but he had been met with great resistance. He tendered his resignation and went to Azusa Street to meet God. God asked him if he was willing to give up everything, including preaching. Reluctantly, he told God he wanted the fullness of the Spirit more than he wanted to pastor a church. Suddenly, he was filled with the Spirit. A British Indian asked him, "How did you learn my mother tongue?" The pastor was dumbfounded, "I do not know your mother tongue." The man responded, "This is the first time I have heard my mother tongue since I left India."[21]

That pastor's wife was sure he had become an unhinged fanatic. She threatened to leave him and take their three year old baby. Taking the baby he loved in his arms, he pleaded with his wife to go to the meeting with him. "I will go with you one time," she responded. Her bags were packed. She was already emotionally disengaged.

That night, the Holy Spirit was moving in a powerful way. The pastor's wife walked up the aisle in the midst of the prayer and praise, still uncertain that such passion was from God. But in that moment, the glory of God broke over her soul. She lifted her hands and was filled with the Spirit. One week later, A. G. Garr, and his wife were headed to India with no sending agency, no support, just propelled by the Holy Spirit like hundreds of others in the early days of Azusa Street.

The First Missionaries

The call to fellowship with fire, to live in the middle, is missional. It cannot merely be sustained in a static manner. It is an anointing meant to engage, as in ministry, not merely entertain us momentarily.

When Pastor Garr announced his intention to go to India, in obedience to the Spirit, people all over the room began to stand and offer support – five hundred dollars, two hundred dollars, one hundred dollars. In fifteen minutes, there was enough money to get a party of five to India with the message of Pentecost. Three weeks later, he was headed to India. Later, Garr would pastor a thriving church in Charlotte, North Carolina – Garr Memorial Church.

From Azusa Street, many began rushing off to all corners of

the globe to spread the news. By September 1906, only months after the initial outpouring, scores of evangelists were moving up and down the west coast – San Jose, San Francisco, and San Diego, to Salem and Portland, and to Spokane and Seattle. By December 1906, meetings were being held in Denver and Colorado Springs, in Indianapolis and Minneapolis, in Akron, Alliance, and Cleveland, Ohio. There were meetings in Chattanooga, in Norfolk, and even in New York City.

By the end of 1906, at least thirteen missionaries had been sent to Africa. Four were white. Nine were African-Americans, who were soon joined by three more, in a mission to Liberia. By January, 1907, additional ministries traceable to Azusa Street could be found in Monrovia, Mexico, Canada, Western Europe, the Middle East, West Africa, and several countries in Asia. By 1908, the movement had spread to South Africa, Central and Eastern Europe, and even Northern Russia. Azusa street was a missionary enterprise opened by God. The fullness of the Spirit, the call to fellowship with fire, is about being in the middle.

In May, 1907, the *Apostolic News* would report:

Pentecostal power is sweeping its way into churches, missions, asylums, jails, hospitals, and soldiers barracks. People are being cleansed by the Blood of Jesus and the power of the Holy Ghost. The saints of the Lord from Los Angeles to Africa and India are speaking in tongues and glorifying God.[22]

They never felt they were the zenith of some final and ultimate movement, only the beginning of what was to be a complete reformation of the Church, a renewal of the whole body in the power of the Spirit, to complete a global mission. In the October, 1906, issue is this declaration: "We are only in the A.B.C. of this wonderful power of God that is to sweep over the world."[23] And the outpouring was more about mission than experience. From the beginning, it was more global than personal. It transcended Los Angeles and quickly touched the world.

In India, one reporter stumbled on what he called "an extraordinary religious manifestation, as remarkable as anything in connection with the great revival in Wales." He simply chose to "narrate, soberly and consecutively, what I have seen and heard concerning this 'baptism with fire' and pouring out of 'the gift of tongues,' whereby ignorant Hindu girls speak in Sanskrit, Hebrew, Greek, English, and other languages as yet unidentified."[24]

It was happening all over the world. The *Apostolic Faith* publication, which chronicled the happenings at Azusa Street, soon had 50,000 subscribers from around the world.[25] From Azusa Street, Pentecostalism, inflaming hearts and emboldening believers, spread rapidly throughout the earth and began its advance toward becoming a major force in Christendom.

At the Half-Century

David du Plessis was in his office in Johannesburg early in the morning in December, 1936. He was serving as the General Secretary for the Apostolic Faith Mission (AFM). And he was host to the legendary Smith Wigglesworth. He was to be the interpreter for Wigglesworth for the annual conference of the AFM. (Barbara and I hosted David for a series of meetings in Fresno, California in the 1970s and heard this story from him first hand.)

Early one morning, Wigglesworth burst into his office. David recalled rising to meet him, but Wigglesworth pressed him against the wall and immediately began to prophesy. "At the turn of the half-century," he declared, "God will visit the mainline denominations with an outpouring of the Holy Spirit." Wigglesworth abruptly left the office. The whole experience, du Plessis would reflect later, seemed a bit strange.

No one in that day, given the rejection, the extreme resistance of Catholics and Protestants to the Pentecostal message, thought there would ever be an embrace of the Pentecostal experience by the whole of Christendom. Wigglesworth predicted a Pentecostal movement, eclipsing anything that had previously happened, including Azusa Street.

He prayerfully offered one piece of advice to du Plessis – humility. And it was a critical key to David's success. He would refer to himself as "God's little donkey," his role to only bring a message.

Minutes after the encounter, Wigglesworth came to breakfast as if he were greeting David for the first time that morning. He inquired about how David was doing. "Very puzzled," David replied, referencing the earlier encounter. Wigglesworth then told him he had seen a vision in the night, before dawn. He predicted fields full of people, buildings being unable to hold them, all hungry for direct encounters with God, for the fullness of the Spirit. He confessed to David, that he knew Pentecostals did not expect such a thing to happen, and that he himself struggled with the vision.

"It will not begin during my lifetime. When I pass away, then you can begin to think about it." He marked the time, as being near the turn of the half-century. Du Plessis said that he did not dwell on the encounter. He did not fully understand it. It was not something that catalyzed him in a personal way or immediately changed the course of his life.

Bringing Unity to Pentecostals

Three weeks after the prophecy, David du Plessis was attending the meeting of the 1937 General Council of the Assemblies of God, held in Memphis, Tennessee. One of the items discussed was a potential meeting of all Pentecostal leaders from around the world. Donald Gee, the great Assembly of God leader, suggested that David could be secretary for such a meeting.[26] That positioned him to convene a larger gathering – the first ever Pentecostal World Conference.

World War II put the meeting on a slow track. The first Pentecostal World Conference (PWC) would finally be held in Zurich, Switzerland, in 1947. Smith Wigglesworth died that year. David du Plessis, traveling with Paul H. Walker, the Church of God World Missions Director, would be involved in a tragic and near fatal accident. But the result would change his life. From his hospital bed, he would organize the 1949 PWC. While in the hospital, God visited him and told him, "It is time for the fulfillment of the word of Wigglesworth." David would attend the PWC on crutches. His teaching position at Lee College in Cleveland, Tennessee, would enable his family to obtain a residence in the United States. While continuing to teach and with the help of students, he would organize the 1952 PWC in London.[27]

The Charismatic Renewal

While the global convening of Pentecostals was a noble thing. God had bigger plans. He wanted no exclusive group representing Him. He wanted all His people to be filled with the Spirit. He wanted to infuse Christendom with priestly power. That is still His desire.

David resigned from his position at Lee College and moved to Stamford, Connecticut. There, he developed a friendship with Dr. John A. Mackay, President of Princeton Theological Seminary. MacKay invited him to attend the World Conference of the International Missionary Council. At that conference, David du Plessis would talk or meet privately with 110 of the 210 delegates, including Dr. Willem Visser 't Hooft, the secretary of the World Council of Churches (WCC). Most had never met a Pentecostal first-hand.

The divide between Protestantism and Pentecostalism was so deep and wide. Dr. Hooft invited David to speak at the second assembly of the WCC in 1954.

He told those global leaders of non-Pentecostal Protestant churches, that Jesus was the Baptizer in the Holy Spirit. He exhibited humility, by confessing wrong attitudes of Pentecostals toward non-Pentecostals. His humility was the gift needed to help international leaders acknowledge their own prejudices. Forgiveness ever after became a cornerstone of his message. But such a sword is double edged. Pentecostals, who had been forced from Protestant churches, persecuted and treated with ridicule, did not feel such an apology was appropriate. If anything, the mainline churches should apologize. Du Plessis was both disarmed by the warm reception and hunger of the mainline churches for the Spirit and was unprepared for rejection by his peers.

Pentecostal Catholics

At a subsequent meeting of the WCC in St. Andrews, Scotland, Bernard Leeming, a Roman Catholic priest from Oxford, England, would ask David to pray for him to be baptized in the Holy Spirit. This was the start of the charismatic outpouring of the Spirit among Roman Catholics.

Leeming had connections with the Vatican. He was so overwhelmed by God's renewal in his own life that he arranged for David to meet Pope John in Rome. The journey was just the beginning – and simultaneously, the ending. Du Plessis' head was spinning with open doors to share the Pentecostal message, doors he had never imagined would or could open. The prophecy of Wigglesworth was unfolding. He met Dr. Robert Murray, and subsequently, Dr. Thomas Strandsky, who served as the secretary for the Promotion of Christian Unity for the Catholics. Strandsky had been searching for a Pentecostal with whom he could have open dialogue. He had also been told that David du Plessis might be the one Pentecostal with whom he could and should meet.[28]

While David was finding doors wide open in Rome, his Pentecostal brothers were aghast, horrified at his actions. Tragically, they had assumed that they had been given "an exclusive" on the Pentecostal experience. They acted as if they owned "the Holy Spirit." They alone, they seemed to suggest, had been given a franchise on the fire. Israel was called by God to secure the middle and invite the nations to join them. Pentecostals had been initiated into the Spirit to model the Spirit-infused life, and then to invite others to be filled with the Spirit. The middle can never be exclusive. It belongs to all God's people. He wants every believer to know him - personally, to walk and talk with Him, in order to reach the unreached. He wants all filled with the Spirit, that they might call the dead to life.

Suddenly, David would find himself alone. He would be virtually expelled from the Pentecostal movement. For almost two decades, he would walk apart from his brothers in classical Pentecostal churches. They struggled not only to understand him, but also to understand how the rest of Christendom could be authentically "Pentecostal" without leaving their historic churches and joining the Pentecostal movement. God, obviously, wanted a Pentecostal witness inside of every movement, a group of Spirit-filled believers "in the middle" of every segment of Christianity. Du Plessis would find himself in the vortex of spiritual warfare - in the strategic middle.

His position was not comfortable. He would walk alone - and be misunderstood by almost all classical Pentecostal leaders for a season. While his Pentecostal brothers misunderstood him, the Catholics would quickly learn that he was no push-over. Cardinal Bea, Standsky's supervisor, asked David, "What do the Pentecostals want to say to Rome?" David paused. "The Pentecostals have no intention of talking to Rome," he boldly declared. Without displaying sentiment, Bea asked David, "What do you want to say to Rome?" David answered courageously, "Make the Bible available to every Catholic in the world in his own language. The Holy Spirit will make that book come alive and that will change lives and renew the church." Bea was surprised. Then he responded, "That is what the Holy Father wants to know, write it down," he said to his secretary.

In 1964, David was invited to be an observer at the historic Vatican Council. In Switzerland in 1972, the first of ten "Dialogues" between Catholics and Pentecostals, including Charismatics, took place. In 1974, Catholic and Protestant editors named eleven 'shapers and shakers' of the Christian faith. David du Plessis was on the list.[29]

Pentecost would invade every denomination in the late '60's and '70's – Episcopalians, Lutherans, Presbyterians, Methodists, Baptists. Most denominations would establish an official office for charismatic renewal. Stadiums would be full, as Wigglesworth had prophesied, with hungry hearts, longing to be filled with the Spirit. Suddenly, the Pentecostal experience could no longer be associated with a small group of denominations – it was global and diverse, it involved the whole church, the entire body of Christ. Now 80 percent of world Pentecostals are in traditionally non-Pentecostal churches.

A Century Later – The Renewal of the Middle

A century after Azusa Street, the movement has 600 million adherents – or more. It is the fastest growing segment of Christianity – "growing at the rate of nine million per year."[30] Harvey Cox has suggested that the movement will double, expanding to 1.2 billion, becoming the largest segment of Christendom.[31] The movement, only a hundred years old, has become a worldwide phenomenon. And yet, it should be clear, that it is much more than an experience. It is the call of God, upon the whole of the Church, to come to the middle.

Six-hundred million Pentecostals and Charismatics trace their roots to the humble origins of Azusa Street, 100 years ago, in a beat-up Los Angeles mission. Five years before the Azusa Street, an outpouring in Topeka had occurred on Stone Avenue, at Bethel Bible School. On January 1, 1901, in the first hour of the new century, Agnes Ozman was filled with the Spirit. She spoke Chinese for three days. She was so enraptured, that she could not speak in English. Soon, others were filled with the Spirit.

This call to the middle, at the turn of the century, launched the greatest expansion in global missions ever! Seventy-percent of all those who have come to Christ since A.D. 100, have come since Azusa Street. Pentecostal empowerment and witness go hand-in-hand. The fullness of the Spirit is not an addition to salvation, nor is it an experiential trinket. It is an anointing to participate in the ministry of Jesus, an anointing for priestly ministry from the middle. No one is to be is excluded. It is a call, to enjoin every nation and tribe, every tongue and kindred, with the good news of Christ, by everyone now in his Church – everyone.

> Anybody, regardless of their age – could be six or they could be 60 – it didn't matter whether they were black or white or brown or any other color – didn't matter what their level of education was – didn't matter what their gender was – they were understood to be a real priesthood of all believers in which every believer had something to give, something to contribute...[32]

That, according to Cecil Robeck, Azusa Street historian.

The Pentecostal Drift Away from the Middle

If there is a tragedy, it is this. One hundred years after Azusa Street, Pentecostal congregations now evidence little difference from non-Pentecostal churches. Pentecostal people have moved from the middle, back to the end. Pentecostals have retained an appetite for high-powered pastors or evangelist-type preachers to pray for them! But they have forgotten how to pray through for themselves. Living from Sunday-to-Sunday, the inner artesian well of Spirit-led living and praying is dry. They draw water from a Sunday cistern and live anemic lives. Lacking personal victory, how can they pray for others? Lacking a vibrant testimony, they have no fresh news of a living God to proclaim to despairing friends. They follow signs when signs should follow them. They listen to the stories of their grandparent's generation as if the ideas are strange and foreign. They are simultaneously hungry for God and fearful of embarrassing revival outbreaks in a now orderly, but dead church. They are skeptical seekers - probably the least likely place for renewal in the city. They are comfortable on the end. Only a hundred years after their institutional birth, they are already lukewarm.

> *We are come with the rising of the day. The road before is plain, but we must ride warily, for war is abroad. Do not sleep. Draw no weapon. Speak no haughty word.*[33]

God is now looking for people who will move to the middle! Israel wrongly assumed that no one could replace them, but we Gentiles, were grafted into the tree (Romans 11:19f). Paul warned that we must not now assume an exclusive right. After all, Jesus declared that God could raise up to Abraham children from the stones (Matthew 3:9). When the charismatic movement took place, many Pentecostals were offended. How could the Methodists be filled with the Spirit? The Episcopalians? The Lutherans? – and so on! It was as if the franchise rights to Spirit-Baptism had been infringed upon.

Pentecostals incubated apostolic gifts, but God wanted genuine Spirit-filled believers in every tribe. He never intended to make an exclusive movement out of Pentecost. It was and is His intent to empower all believers. In the days of the Charismatic Renewal, He sent fresh fire into every denominational tribe, first to renew that tribe, but then to reach the nations with the gospel. We assumed that we, the Spirit-filled churches, were His people! And others were – well, not his people, unless they joined us. He was much more loving and inclusive than we were willing to be. At the turn of the half-century, He began to invade his multi-denominational church with the power of the Holy Spirit.

It is still His desire to fill every Christ-exalting, people-loving believer, with the power of the Holy Spirit so that they can be equipped to do what He called them to do – share the living, resurrected and enthroned Christ with lost friends and family.

---

[1] Tolkien, *The Lord of the Rings: The Return of the King*, 20.
[2] Ibid, 145.
[3] Ibid, 154.
[4] William G. McLoughlin, *Is There a Third Force in Christendom?* (Daedalus, Vol. 96, No. 1, Religion in America; Winter, 1967), 43-68.
[5] Cecil M. Robeck, *The Azusa Street Mission and Revival: The Birth of the Global Pentecostal* (Nashville, TN: Thomas Nelson, 2006), 149.
[6] Andrew Newberg and Mark Robert Waldman, *Born to Believe: God, Science, and the Origin of Ordinary and Extraordinary* (New York, NY: Free Press, 2006), 192.
[7] www.upstreamca.org/azusastrevival.html.
[8] Robert R. Owens, *The Azusa Street Revival* (Xulon Press; 2005), 94.
[9] Tolkien, *The Hobbit* (New York: Ballantine Books, 1982), 303.
[10] Frank Bartleman, Quoted by Roger K. Price, *So You Want to Be a Missionary?* (Authorhouse; 2007), 127.
[11] Roebuck, 159.
[12] Roberts Liardon, *The Azusa Street Revival: When the Fire Fell-An*

In-Depth Look at the People (Shippensburg, PA; Destiny Image, 2006), 100.
13 T. J. Saxby, *When the Spirit comes: Christian revivals around the world* (Multiply Publications), 52.
14 Roebuck, 141.
15 Cecil Roebuck, *The Colorline Was Washed Away in the Blood: A Pentecostal Dream for Racial Harmony* (Christian Education Press, 1995).
16 *LA Times*, September, 1906.
17 Roebuck, *The Azusa Street Mission*, 9.
18 Ibid, 217f.
19 Vinson Synan, *The Holiness-Pentecostal Tradition: Charismatic Movements in the Twentieth Century*, (Grand Rapids, MI: William B. Eerdmans, 1971, 1997), 103-104.
20 enrichmentjournal.ag.org/200602/200602_142_Legacies.cfm.
21 www.cbn.com/cbnnews/cwn/122906 Azusa2006.aspx.
22 ifphc.wordpress.com/2007/03/01/the-azusa-street-papers.
23 www.christianitytoday.com/ch/news/2005/sep8.html.
24 *The Apostolic Faith*, Vol. I. No. 2; Los Angeles, Cal., October, 1906.
25 Vinson Synan, *The Century of the Holy Spirit* (Thomas Nelson Publishers, 2001).
26 www.jonasclark.com/david_duplessis.htm
27 Ibid.
28 Ibid.
29 Ibid.
30 en.wikipedia.org/wiki/Charismatic_movement – 63k.
31 Harvey Cox, *Fire from Heaven* (Da Capa Press, 1995).
32 Cecil Robeck, *The Azusa Street Mission and Revival*.
33 Tolkien, *The Lord of the Rings: The Two Towers*, 117.

Discussion Guide

1. In the early days after the Azusa Street outpouring, the meetings ran 24/7. What would it be like to be in a non-stop revival like Azusa Street?

2. The revival at Azusa Street seems so different than modern revival outbreaks – at least in this sense. Azusa seemed saturated in humility and anonymity, brokenness and repentance. Why are modern revivals not piecing calls to repentance and humility? Can such 'revivals' really impact the culture?

3. What is the difference between a 'manifestation' revival and an humbling, transformational revival?

4. When is the last time you were in a meeting where a 'siege of silence' came over the congregation? What is the significance of such moments?

5. How significant was it that the revival came first among blacks in a city that was promoting Aryanism? How significant is that the meeting soon became multi-ethnic?

6. Is our witness diminished by our continued segregation in worship – black congregations, white or Hispanic, Asian or Indian?

7. "The color line has been washed away by the blood!" Why is that not true now?

8. Azusa Street quickly became a mission-sending agency. How are Pentecost and Mission connected?

9. Why do you think traditional Pentecostals reacted so strongly

to mainline denominations and Catholic Christians when they began to experience Holy Spirit encounters?

10. Do you think we see Spirit-fullness as a kind of super-salvation or as it is intended, an anointing to do ministry? An enduement of power for service?

GANDALF: *"Over the bridge! Fly! This is a foe beyond any of you. I must hold the narrow way. Fly! "*

Gandalf stood in the middle of the span, leaning on the staff...His enemy halted...the shadow reached out like two vast wings. It raised the whip, and the thongs whined and cracked. Fire came from its nostrils. But Gandalf still firm.

GANDALF TO THE DRAGON: *"You cannot pass."*

The orcs stood still, and a dead silence fell.

GANDALF: *"I am a servant of the Secret Fire, wielder of the flame of Anor. You cannot pass. The dark fire will not avail you, flame of Udum. Go back to the Shadow. You cannot pass."*

The Balrog made no answer. The fire in it seemed to die, but the darkness grew. It stepped forward slowly on the bridge, and drew iteself to a great height, and its wings were spread from wall to wall. Gandalf seemed small, altogether alone, grey and bent, like a wizened tree before the onset of a storm. From out of the shadow a red sword leaped flaming. There was a ringing clash and a stab of white fire.

GANDALF: *"You shall not pass!"*[1]

SECTION TWO
Jesus Teaches on the Middle

GANDALF: *"We must press our Enemy, and no longer wait upon him for the move.[2] If it is not countered swiftly, I deem that the City will be lost ere ten days be gone."*[3]

ARAGORN: *"I have no help to send, there I must go myself. But there is only one way through the mountains that will bring me to the coastlands before all is lost. That is the Paths of the Dead."*[4]

ARAGORN: *"Three days. But I see that it cannot now be hastened."* He looked up, and it seemed that he had made some decision; his face was less troubled. *"Then, by your leave, lord, I must take new counsel for myself and my kindred. We must ride our own road, and no longer in secret. For me the time of stealth has passed. I will ride east by the swiftest way, and I will take the Paths of the Dead."*

THEODEN: *"The Paths of the Dead?"* Theoden trembled. *"If there be in truth such paths, their gate is in Dunharrow; but no living man may pass it. If you seek the Paths of the Dead then our parting is come, and it is little likely that we shall ever meet again under the Sun."*

ARAGORN: *"But I say to you, that in battle we may yet meet again,"* declared Aragorn.[5] *"And now our fates are woven together."*[6]

no justice. We rarely connect either the presence or absence of prayer with the state of justice in our community. With the middle abandoned, there was no justice and no salvation – no redemptive activity,

> *Jesus' life was a life of prayer. And He wanted that to be true of His disciples.*

no consistent representation of God in the earth or of man from the earth to God. Prayer is the precondition for salvation-action. Redemption begins in prayer. Salvation processes are rooted in prayer. Without an intercessor, Israel was scattered and dominated by Babylon. What a picture. *"Therefore His own arm brought salvation."* He chose to come to earth, through the incarnation, in order to heal the gap that had occurred by the fall of man, the gap in the middle, and from that middle to intercede for mankind from the earth. Jesus came to the earth - to pray. Man had been created for communion with God, for unbroken fellowship with the Divine. And on the basis and strength of that inherent and spiritual bond, he was given a representative role and empowered with dominion. Created in the very image of God, he was designed for the role in the middle. But the communion and the communication between heaven and earth, through the kingly and priestly Adam, was irrevocably shattered by sin.

Jesus, the last Adam – not the second or third, for there could never be another, since he was mankind's only hope – came to restore that communion. He came to reinstate dominion, first, at the spiritual and moral levels. He came to the earth to pray – as a man. He began his ministry in prayer (Matthew 4:1-3). He ended his earthly ministry in prayer (Matthew 26:36-45). Jesus withdrew from his disciples and the crowds to be alone to pray. He often went up on a mountainside or to a solitary or lonely place to pray. When the disciples arose in the morning, at times, he had already gone out to find a place of prayer (Matthew 14:23, Mark 1:35, 6:46, Luke 5:16). He spent the whole night in prayer before he chose the twelve (Luke 6:12). At the tomb of Lazarus, he thanked the Father for hearing him. He prayed – and Lazarus was raised from the dead (John 11:41-43). Before he fed the thousands, Jesus gave thanks, looking up to heaven (Matthew 14:19, 15:36, Mark 6:41, 8:6, Luke 9:16, John 6:11). The writer of Hebrews offers a powerful descriptive of his prayer life,

> *During the days of Jesus' life on earth, he offered up prayers and petitions with loud cries and tears to the one who could save him from death, and he was heard because of his reverent submission* (Hebrews 5:7, NIV).

His life was a life of prayer. He moved from one place of prayer to another, and then to another, and still to yet another, with the power and wisdom of God flowing out of him in-between. He came to the earth to pray.

His Ministry Was Prayer

He did not pray to find spiritual strength to support his ministry activities. He did not pray in order to preach better or teach more effectively. Prayer was not the *prop* for his ministry. Prayer *was* his ministry. His preaching and teaching, his miracles and ministry to people, flowed out of prayer. His insights and the direction to share them came from seasons with the Father. John 5:30 records his words, *"I can of Myself do nothing. As I hear (prayer), I judge."* In John 15:15, he said *"... things that I heard from My Father I have made known to you."*

Many in ministry, place preaching, teaching, or ministry activity at the heart of their endeavors. We are an action-oriented culture. So we see prayer as the means by which we gain spiritual strength to do ministry. We pray to invite God's blessing on our actions and to secure his favor. We have it backwards. Ministry *activity* is not the main thing. *Relationship* is the main thing. It is actually our relationship with God, evidenced by constant prayerful dependence upon Him, which makes effective ministry possible. Without a relationship with Him, how can we help people? In truth, our helping is His helping through us. If Jesus could "do nothing" without dependence on the Father, how can we accomplish a divine mandate with human strength? If he only spoke what he heard the Father say, why do we continue to substitute a *good* word for *God's* word to his people? Prayer is not a nice and sweet thing; it is an essential and necessary thing. Prayer is – our ministry. Our calling is to spend time with God (Mark 3:13-14). Everything else flows out of that.

Jesus not only came to the earth to pray – he is praying now. Hebrews 7:25 says, *"He is also able to save to the uttermost those who come to God through Him, since He always lives to make intercession for them."* If we are going to be like Jesus, we must become intercessors! Prayer must become the essence of our Christian life.

Jesus' life was a life of prayer. And he wanted that to be true of his disciples. So, not only did he retreat to certain places to pray, but he took his disciples with him - to pray. He wanted to infect them with prayer passion. When is the last time you called someone or they called you and said, "Let's get away and pray together?" Christians go to crusades and revival meetings together, to gospel concerts, plays and pageants together, but it is rare for the typical Christian to gather friends for a prayer meeting.

A Gathering Crowd in the Middle

In this passage, Jesus goes to one of his favorite places of prayer and takes his disciples with him.

Intercession – The Uncomfortable Strategic Middle

As a young 22 year-old evangelist, Billy Graham was on a trip, when he heard Stephen Olford talk about being filled with the Spirit. The young evangelist approached the Welshman and humbly admitted that he longed for a deeper anointing of the Spirit in his life. Olford agreed to spend a couple days with Billy. They would meet and talk during the day, and Graham would preach at night. In a small stone hotel, Olford led Graham step-by-step through Biblical passages about the fullness of the Spirit. Something needed to happen. Billy knew it. The crowds were small and passive. His preaching was quite ordinary. Olford emphasized in the private daily meetings, the need for brokenness. He told him that his own life had to be completely turned inside-out, to receive an anointing of God's quickening power. Graham's eyes filled with tears. "That's what I want. That's what I need in my life!" he confessed. Both men knelt and went to prayer. They wept together. They laughed. Olford recalls, "I can still hear Billy pouring out his heart in a prayer of total dedication to the Lord." Graham, Olford said, paced back and forth in the room. At one point he exclaimed that his heart "was flooded with the Holy Spirit." That prayer meeting changed the ministry of Billy Graham. Those in the audience that night would say, "Something has happened to Billy Graham. The world is going to hear from this man."[8]

You catch prayer! You and I are infected by the fever of intercession raging in the heart of another. We learn to pray by being in the middle of passionate prayer meetings. Get around an intercessor when they are experiencing the burden of the Lord. Listen to them groan in the Spirit. See their tears and their brokenness. Sense their agony in prayer. It is contagious. Their spirit permeates a prayer meeting, and others leave with prayer-fire in their heart. Jesus was first and foremost an intercessor. The disciples caught prayer from him.

We often see prayer as a solo experience. In the garden, Jesus sought solitude, and yet not absolute solitude. He took his disciples with him into the garden to pray, and then he removed himself for privacy. Here is tempered solitude. Here is privacy in prayer in the context of a fellowship of praying brothers.

Why is it rare for us to seek others with whom we might get away to pray? When is the last time you invited someone to join you in prayer at your favorite spot? For over 12 years, I led pastors' prayer summits. Pastors from across a city from all denominations would gather in some location out of town for three to four days of prayer – not for teaching or training, but to pray. Sadly, most pastors found such invitations strange. Evidently, the disciples did not find the invitation of Jesus to join him in prayer a bizarre thing at all.

They all prayed in some proximity one to another and to Jesus. The disciples apparently finished praying before Jesus concluded his encounter with the Father. Their prayer sessions weren't very enduring. Having grown silent, evidently, they found themselves listening to him pray. It must have become compellingly clear to them – they didn't pray like he prayed. At this point, *"One of His disciples said to Him, 'Lord, teach us to pray.'"* John had taught his disciples to pray, according to Luke. Not to preach, but to pray. Not to baptize, but to be immersed in intercession. Our priorities are wrong. Our training programs have ignored prayer. Our Bible colleges and seminaries have not even offered a single class on prayer. We have forgotten to pray. We, like the disciples, don't know how to pray. The humble request of the disciples is followed by a powerful teaching moment.

The Prayer Training Program of Jesus

What Jesus gives us here, recorded by Luke, is a complete training program in prayer.

In Luke 11:1-2, he offers *the experience of prayer*. Prayer is first caught, only then it is taught. Second, he gives them an outline, *a template for prayer*. Third, he tells a *story* loaded with *prayer principles*. Fourth, he *amplifies on the principles* in the story, by teaching. Finally, he offers *graduate level principles* on interference issues in prayer. Let's look at each of these.

First, Jesus allows his disciples to *experience prayer*. He allows them to experience a deficit in their own praying. He doesn't teach into a need that they don't realize they have. He cultivates a hunger in them for prayer – by exposing them to the experience of his praying.

Second, he offers *a model* for prayer. What follows is Luke's version of what we have traditionally called "The Lord's Prayer." In truth, it is "the disciple's prayer," our prayer. It is both a prayer to be repeated, and a template for prayer. The prayer can be prayed multiple times in less than a minute. But endless repetition isn't the goal of praying.

The rabbi's used "Index Prayers." They were common among the Jewish people. The words of the prayer were meant to be memorized, but each line then became the clue for extended, extemporaneous praying. Jesus is offering a model to be used, but deeply personalized. Index prayers provided a kind of outline for Spirit-led, Bible-based praying.

> *Our Father in heaven, hallowed be Your name. Your kingdom come. Your will be done on earth as it is in heaven. Give us day by day our daily bread. And forgive us our sins, for we also forgive everyone who is indebted to us. And do not lead us into temptation, but deliver us from the evil one.*

Luke's version omits the doxology - "for thine is the kingdom and the power and the glory forever and ever! Amen." Matthew includes it. Don't doubt for a moment the validity of such a wonderful conclusion to the prayer. Luke's omission is a mystery.

Notice the details of the prayer. Never once in the prayer do you find "me," "my" or "I." Instead, you find "us," "our" and "we." I can't pray without including you. No one can pray without thinking of others. This is not a prayer to be prayed from *the end,* but a prayer to be prayed from *the middle.* It is not an *exclusive* encounter with God, but an *inclusive* encounter that connects God, through me, to others.

The whole prayer is from the middle position. It is as if we were praying for the whole world – "Let your kingdom break into our time-space world." This is a cosmic prayer. It is much bigger than our typical prayers. We are often consumed with praying our narrow slice of pain. Here, prayer is the opening of some celestial doorway that invites God's reign into an otherwise tormented and tumultuous world. It is by this prayer, that physical needs are met – daily bread; that emotional and relational gaps are healed – forgiveness; that the hand of the Evil One is stayed – and in the spiritual dimension of tests or temptations to sin, we find grace to sustain and holiness of heart.

Model One

The prayer is so simple. It is easily outlined into three sections, each with three movements.[9] But we dare not rush through the extraordinary preamble that serves as a frame for the entire prayer encounter – "Our Father, who are in heaven, holy..." Here, intimacy, 'Our Father,' is juxtaposed against his eternal existence, 'who art' - beyond and outside the bounds of time; 'in heaven' - outside the bounds of space, in another dimension; 'holy' - utterly other, unlike earthlings, incomparable, unknowable without self-disclosure. Here is intimacy (Father) and laced with transcendence. Though implicit in the prayer, it demands a delicate

Intercession – The Uncomfortable Strategic Middle

balance between God, as Father – intimacy as possible; and God, as the Holy One, beyond time and space, past finding out. This framework for prayer never fades, we can never leave it – intimacy and transcendence!

In the body of the prayer, the first concern is the *"Glory"* of the Father, then the *"Good"* of the Father's family, and finally the *"Great Certainty"* of the Father's claim in the earth.

GLORY – With regard to the Father's glory, three worshipful petitions are offered:

1. We are to pray that the *name* of God will be revered... "Hallowed by thy name!"

2. We pray that the *rule* of God will be established..."Thy Kingdom come!"

3. We are to pray that the *will* of God will be done..."Thy will be done on earth, as it is in heaven!"

GOOD – With regard to our prayerful concern for good in the Father's family, we offer three petitions:

1. We pray for daily *provision*..."Give us this day our daily bread"

2. We pray for daily *pardon*..."Forgive us our debts, as we forgive our debtors."

3. We pray for daily *protection*... "Lead us not into temptation, but deliver us from evil"

GREAT CERTAINTY – With regard to the great certainty of the Father's redemptive claim, we make three prayerful declarations:

1. We declare that the *Kingdom* belongs to God. The earth is the Lord's. The outcome of all things is now settled... *"For Thine is the Kingdom."*

2. We declare that all *power* comes from God. All authority is resident in God..."And the power ..."

3. We declare finally, that all **glory** is due God! ..."*And the glory...forever!*"

Model Two

Here is yet another outline for the prayer. This one takes the prayer, phrase-by-phrase and expands on each movement:

1. **Pray Fraternally** – Matthew 6:9. *"Our Father"* we are united in family ties to all Christians.

2. **Pray Reverently** – Matthew 6:9. *"Hallowed be thy name."* Let no word pass our lips which in any way that takes the name of God in vain. Soren Kierkegaard said,

    > I cannot pray in the name of Jesus to have my own will; the name of Jesus is not a signature of no importance, but the decisive factor. The fact that the name of Jesus comes at the beginning does not make it a prayer in the name of Jesus; but this means to pray in such a manner that I dare name Jesus in it, that is to say, dare to think of him, think his holy will together with whatever I am praying for.[10]

3. **Pray Loyally and Hopefully** – Matthew 6:10. *"Thy king-dom come!"* While we are permitted to be lovingly familiar, we must be loyally true.

4. **Pray Submissively and Aggressively** – Matthew 6:10. *"Thy will be done."* His will is law, and it is never violated. Such is the standard we should have before us, and we should be satisfied with nothing less.

5. **Pray Dependently** – Matthew 6:11. *"Give us this day our daily bread."* The word *"daily"* has in it no thought of time. It means *"needed"* and *"necessary."* We are not limited to a prayer a day.

Intercession – The Uncomfortable Strategic Middle

6. **Pray Cautiously** – Matthew 6:13. *"Lead us not into temptation, but deliver us from the Evil One."* We should keep as far from danger as possible.[11]

Model Three

Here is another way to pray this prayer. You pray though the relationships in the prayer. Notice all the relationships implied in the prayer:

1. **God, as Father**...*Our Father.*
2. **God, as the utterly Exalted One**...*Who art in heaven.*
3. **God, as the utterly, Holy One**...*Hallowed by thy name.*
4. **God, as King**...*Thy kingdom come.*
5. **God, as the interested Sovereign**...*Thy will be done, on earth as in heaven.*
6. **God, as Provider**...*Give us this day, our daily bread.*
7. **God, as Judge/Forgiver**...*Forgive us our sins.*
8. **God, as Protector and Guide**...*Lead us not into temptation.*
9. **God, as Deliverer and Warrior**...*Deliver us from the Evil One.*
10. **God, as Powerful King**...*For Thine is the kingdom and the power.*
11. **God, as the Object of worship**...*And the glory.*
12. **God, as the Eternal One**...*Forever and ever.*

Prayer is about relationship. The middle demands it. There are more outlines for the praying the "Lord's Prayer" than are imaginable. The bottom line of all of them is that prayer involves form – and yet, the best praying is beyond form. It requires fire – personal passion.

---

1 Tolkien, *The Lord of the Rings: The Two Towers*, 370-371.
2 Tolkien, *The Lord of the Rings: The Return of the King*, 43.

3 Ibid.
4 Ibid.
5 Tolkien, *The Lord of the Rings: The Return of the King,* 41.
6 Ibid, 42.
7 Tolkien, *The Lord of the Rings: Fellowship of the Ring,* Chapter 2.
8 *The Leadership Secrets of Billy Graham,* 22-24.
9 This wonderful and simple outline is not my own. I picked this up "somewhere" and cannot recall or determine the original source. Forgiveness is begged from the author and God is offered praise.
10 Soren Kierkegaard, *The Prayers of Kierkegaard* (The University of Chicago Press: Chicago, ILL; 1956), 212.
11 Amzi Clarence Dixon, Sermon: *"How to Pray."*

Discussion Guide

1. Talk about the idea of a dedicated 'place of prayer' – a prayer room. Does anyone in your study group have one?
2. What would a prayer room/closet look like? What would be in one? Why have one?
3. Jesus came to the earth 'to pray!' Agree or disagree? Prayer was his primary ministry! Agree or disagree?
4. The 'fall of man' had created 'the gap' between God and man, heaven and earth. Intercession fills that gap! Agree or disagree?
5. What happens when the gap is left vacant? Are there gaps in your community that are vacant?
6. "You 'catch' prayer!" Agree or disagree. If that is the case, does your church offer enough opportunities to 'catch prayer?'
7. Both John and Jesus taught their disciples to pray. What does imply about a discipleship process? Are you a disciple only if and when you learn to pray?
8. Have folks share their most meaningful prayer experiences.
9. Jesus took his disciples with him, to pray with them – do you have a prayer partner? Are you a part of a small group of prayer? What is the value of such groups?
10. Talk about the concept of 'index prayers.' Have you tried that as a method of prayer, using the Scripture as a guide?

Frodo: *"I wish it need not have happened in my time."*

Gandalf: *"So do I, and so do all who live to see such times. But that is not for them to decide. All we have to decide is what to do with the time that is given us. And already, Frodo, our time is beginning to look black. For however the fortune of war shall go, may it not so end that much that was fair and wonderful shall pass forever out of Middle-earth? It may. The evil of Sauron cannot be wholly cured, nor made as if it had not been. But to such days we are doomed. Let us now go on with the journey we have begun! Other evils there are that may come; for Sauron is himself but a servant or emissary. Yet it is not our part to master all the tides of the world, but to do what is in us for the succor of those years wherein we are set, uprooting the evil in the fields we know, so that those who live after may have clean earth to till. What weather they shall have is not ours to rule… Sauron knows all this…therefore he is now in great doubt… Too seldom has he been challenged since he returned to his Tower."* [1]

CHAPTER SEVEN
THE STORY OF THE FRIEND IN THE MIDDLE

The Story of the Friend in the Middle

Let's review – Jesus takes his disciples into a prayer experience with him. They pray together. They hear him pray. They ask, "Teach us to pray!" Then, he gives them a model for prayer.

The third thing Jesus does is to tell a story. He teaches about prayer by using a real life illustration. He wants us to see prayer in the context of everyday life.

> And He said to them, "Which of you shall have a friend, and go to him at midnight and say to him, 'Friend, lend me three loaves; for a friend of mine has come to me on his journey, and I have nothing to set before him'; and he will answer from within and say, 'Do not trouble me; the door is now

shut, and my children are with me in bed; I cannot rise and give to you?' I say to you, though he will not rise and give to him because he is his friend, yet because of his persistence he will rise and give him as many as he needs" (Luke 11:5-8).

Let's pick the story up in the middle.

The Inconvenient Middle

You are the host. A friend of yours, an acquaintance, perhaps a relative, is alone at night in the city in which you live. He has no money for shelter or for bread to eat. He is destitute. Hungry and vulnerable, alone and penniless, he remembers that you live in the city. About midnight, he knocks on your door. Everyone knows, a call at midnight is rarely good news!

You glance outside. You recognize your friend. It may have been years since you last saw him. Still, you open the door. You push aside the inconvenience. You welcome the long lost friend into your home. He quickly tells you his story. He is in need. He has turned to you. Full of compassion, you make a place for him to rest. The whole family is rallied to accommodate the midnight visitor.

Inadequate for the Middle

So far, you have an 'A' for gracious hospitality. Then you sense something amiss in the eyes of your friend. He appears weaker than the journey would have made him. "How long has it been since you have eaten?" you ask. "Too long," he responds without a precise answer. You guess that it might have been days. Now, your empathy has owned the need of your friend in need. His hunger is now your problem. This is the essence of intercession. The need, however, is beyond your capacity. You have no bread in your house. Here again, is the essence of intercession – we empathize prayerfully, offering to God the needs of others, which we ourselves cannot meet. We seek answers, for questions we ourselves cannot answer. We seek breakthroughs, for which we ourselves have no strength.

Julio C. Ruibal was a Columbian preacher whose martyrdom catalyzed a prayer movement in Cali that changed the whole city. He would declare, "Our greatest victories are won on our knees and with empty stomachs."

The Uncomfortable Middle
Back to the Parable

Although you, the host, have no bread, your wealthy neighbor always has bread. He has bread for the day and bread left over. In fact, Jesus begins by emphasizing the quality of the relationship with the friend with plenty. We might paraphrase the question, "Which of you have a friend you can go to for a need at midnight?" The quality of the relationship on both sides is critical - the friend in need feels free enough to show up at midnight. And the strength of the relationship with your friend with plenty frees you to make an imposing request of him at midnight.

Without a hospitable and

> FRODO: As for where I am going, it would be difficult to give that away, for I have no clear idea myself...I have never even considered the direction. For where am I to go? And by what shall I steer? What is to be my quest?
>
> GANDALF: You cannot see very far. Neither can I. It may be your task to find the Cracks of Doom; but that quest may be for others; I do not know.
>
> FRODO: But in the meantime, what course am I to take?
>
> GANDALF: Toward danger; but not too rashly, not too straight.[2]

compassionate heart, your relationship with your needy friend would result in a closed door. And without a quality relationship with your friend with plenty, compassion alone would not have been enough for your friend in need. The subtext is about our need for both a quality relationship with God, and an open inviting relationship to friends around who are in need of the bread of life itself.

> **THEODEN:** Crops can be re-sown, homes re-built. Within these walls...we will outlast them.
>
> **ARAGORN:** They do not come to destroy Rohan's crops or villages. They come to destroy its people. Down to the last child.
>
> **THEODEN:** What will you have me do? Look at my men. Their courage hangs by a thread.[3]

Driven by the need of your traveling friend, you go to your well-heeled neighbor, as if the need was your own. You disturb him. You awaken him. *"Friend, lend me three loaves; for a friend of mine has come to me on his journey, and I have nothing to set before him."* It's midnight. Your affluent friend does not share your enthusiasm for your hungry friend. He is obviously unhappy about your visit. You wait patiently, but his answer is less than encouraging. *"Do not trouble me; the door is now shut, and my children are with me in bed; I cannot rise and give to you?"*

What will you do? This is an important friend. He has connections at city-hall. He is on the board of directors at the bank. He has been a lifesaver to you before. You don't want to lose this relationship! You can't upset him. Not for some distant friend who you have not seen in years and may never see again. You start to walk away from the door. You will tell your guest, "I thought I might get you some bread. I failed. Looks like we will have to wait until the bread markets open in the morning." Surely, you reason, the friend will be okay with that explanation. He understands that you can't risk a secure relationship with another valued friend - for his sake!

Suddenly, you have a change of heart. What if it were you? What if you were the hungry and destitute one? In that moment, your values change, the paradigm shifts. You are not the host of a mere penniless drifter. You cannot sacrifice him to protect the relationship with your rich and well-supplied friend. You become a passionate advocate for the need of the hungry, itinerate friend. You have become an intercessor. You go back to the door of your friend-with-plenty. You now beat on the door. You refuse to be turned away. You are making quite a scene. The whole neighborhood is on the edge of being aroused. You are now banging on the door. You are lifting your voice. You are demanding that you be given bread.

Jesus says,

I say to you, though he will not rise and give to him because he is his friend, yet because of his persistence he will rise and give him as many as he needs.

The relationship with the friend-with-plenty allows the approach of his house at midnight, but the relationship itself is not enough. Your friend will not simply give you bread because he knows you. You must ask. You must do more, you must persist in asking, it seems. You must ask with passion and intensity. And yet, the request cannot be submitted at all without the relationship. And more than a casual, inert relationship is required. You must put a critical demand on the relationship. More than merely and meekly asking is necessary, passion is demanded. Persistence is required. "Asking," Spurgeon said, "is the law of the kingdom!"[4] We must ask with an attitude that says, "We will not and cannot be denied." Someone's life is at stake. Someone needs bread. "I can't – we can't deny them. We won't be turned away." In the passage, the host asked for "a loan of three loaves." But his determination rewarded him with "a gift" of three loaves. What a difference.

> *Prayer builds in a protection against lethal substitutes.*

We may think that God, being good, sees our needs and that he will automatically take care of us. It is not true. God demands that we pray. *"You have not, because you ask not"* (James 4:2). The host asks with intensity and persistence, and as a result, he returns to the house with bread to feed his guest. He will not go to bed hungry.

The Critical and Strategic Middle

This is a powerful picture of intercessory prayer. Prayer here is interfaced with evangelism. There are some felt needs in the lives of the unsaved, that we can meet. There are others that only God can meet. He is the friend with plenty. We are the friend in the middle. All around us are hungry people, looking for the bread that satisfies. We tell ourselves, as lay people, that we can't meet their need. We are not trained to meet their need. It is not our job to meet their need. True – but only in part. Neither can preachers meet their needs. Only God can satisfy the deepest hunger within any of us.

Our role is to embrace the needy in a time a crisis – friends and family, acquaintances and associates. We are to relate in caring ways. We are to meet the needs that can be met by being gracious and compassionate, embracing and listening. And then, we are to go to God, our Friend with plenty, and plead for him to meet their deepest needs – their spiritual hunger. They can't go directly to him. They don't have a relationship with Him. We do. Our relationship with them makes us the critical link for connecting heaven and earth, a holy God and sinners, a loving God and the hurting.

Here are the elements in this story that make for good intercessor-evangelists:

1. **A relationship with people in need** – one that invites a surprise visit at midnight. Most Christians end up, after a few years, cutting off all relationships to non-believers. Most do not have a relationship with the unsaved that invites a surprise visit at midnight. Perhaps God wants us to offer such an open door. Perhaps we need to find a way to make it clear to family and friends, that if they have a need in the middle of the night, they are free to call us. This is the first step toward putting yourself in the uncomfortable, critical and strategic middle.

2. **A gracious reception** – one that makes room. When the sojourning friend rings the doorbell, he is graciously met and warmly received. There is no rebuff. There is no recommendation for a cheap motel nearby. He is not grilled and questioned. He is immediately welcomed. The coffee pot is on. A pallet is laid out. A bed is prepared. His coat is taken. His belongings are stored. He is embraced. This is grace.

3. **A willingness to be inconvenienced by the need of another.** The traveler in Luke 11 does not appear to be a family member. He may not even be a close friend or even a business partner. He appears, at best, to be a recognized chum. And yet, there is no whispering in the background, no resistance, "Why did he come here? Doesn't he have a home? His uncle lives a few blocks over. Why is he putting us out? What responsibility do we have toward him? I have to go to work tomorrow. We have other guests coming in on the weekend How long will he stay? This is terribly inconvenient." It is inconvenient at that. Those who order their lives in rigid and self-serving ways will rarely be used by God in the middle. Ministry to others is rarely convenient. Love always involves a price. Convenience did not save us. The cross did. Expedience did not rescue

us from sin. God the Father reached for us over the dead body of his son, Jesus. A church that demands that God and ministry to others fit into a convenient schedule will not change a warped world and pull men out of the fire. "If Jesus Christ be God, and died for me, then no sacrifice can be too great for me to make for Him," declared C. T. Studd, the great English missionary to India, China and Africa.[5]

4. **Sensitivity and the capacity to empathize with needs** – he must have seen hunger in the eyes of his friend. Self preoccupation will keep us from empathizing with others. It will blind us to any needs but our own. Sensitivity to the needs of others is a grace that demands cultivation in our day. In a me-first, self-centered culture, we close our eyes to pain. "Deal with it" is a favorite expression of people who have no time to invest in others. Therapists abound with practices loaded with clients who only needed a listening friend. Seventy percent of the typical counselor's client-base is people dealing with the problems of living. Without a trusted and empathetic confidant, they pay for one. We insulate ourselves. "Don't get involved!" we tell ourselves. "Don't answer the door," we might have decided, had we been the friend in the middle in our story. Feeling that we cannot meet such needs, we don't even want to hear them. A part of our problem is the cultural pressure to be self-reliant. Listen to culture whisper to us, "Don't put yourself in a situation that is beyond you, past your limits. Don't expose any weakness. Plan to come out a winner. Limit vulnerable moments. Cover your 'Achilles' heel'. Show your best side. Don't let 'em see you cry. Don't ask for advice – that's being weak. Don't ask for anything. Be tough." Such a recipe produces plastic people. Jesus is calling us to open our doors to people whose needs we cannot meet, and to feel their pain. To cry with them. To celebrate possibilities with them. To just be there for them. Ole Kristian Hallesby, the great prayer teacher, would advise us,

Listen, my friend! Your helplessness is your best

prayer. It calls from your heart to the heart of God with greater effect than all your uttered pleas. He hears it from the very moment that you are seized with helplessness, and He becomes actively engaged at once in hearing and answering the prayer of your helplessness.[6]

5. ***Compassion is evident.*** Empathy feels pain, but compassion moves us to respond. Compassion is always at the root of Christ-like actions. William Law observed, "There is nothing that makes us love a man so much as praying for him."[7] Jesus prayed for us. He wept over Jerusalem and at the tomb of Lazarus. Thus, he shed tears in the face of both sin and death. A weeping God demands sons and daughters who weep. Bob Pierce, the founder of World Vision would say, *"Let my heart be broken with the things that break God's heart."*[8] Compassion that is shut up and fails to act, is not love at all. The compassion of the friend in the middle *moves* him. He must *do* something.

6. ***There is bold action.*** True compassion moves us. The friend in the middle will use his relationships to the advantage of his friend in need. Feelings of empathy are not enough. He is moved to act. He will not let his friend go to bed hungry. He himself cannot sleep with the hunger of his friend on his mind. David Livingston, the great missionary to Africa would say, "Sympathy is no substitute for action."[9]

He will persist, risking his relationship with his friend with plenty. "To pray diligently," Luther would say, "is more than half the task."[10] To use Tertullian's phrase, "You should, with a holy conspiracy, besiege heaven."[11] This is what the friend in the middle does. Oswald Chambers believed, "We do not pray at all until we are at our wits end."[12] This man has no other option, but prayer. He prays. He prays passionately. He won't be denied.

Thomas Manton said, "In genuine prayer, humility joins itself to holy audacity and impassioned boldness without contradiction."

Samuel Chadwick declared, "Intensity is a law of prayer. God is found by those who seek Him with all their heart. The fervent effectual prayer of the righteous is of great force."[13] Chadwick believed,

> There is no power like that of prevailing prayer – of Abraham pleading for Sodom, Jacob wrestling in the stillness of the night, Moses standing in the breach, Hannah intoxicated with sorrow, David heart-broken with remorse and grief, Jesus in sweat and blood. Add to this list from the records of the church your personal observation and experience, and always there is cost of passion unto blood. Such prayer prevails. It turns ordinary mortals into men of power. It brings power. It brings fire. It brings rain. It brings life. It brings God.[14]

Rich is the person who has a praying friend. A friend in the middle is invaluable.

---

1. Tolkien, *The Lord of the Rings: The Return of the King*, 160-161.
2. Ibid, 73.
3. www.imdb.com/character/ch0000155/quotes. Accessed May 8, 2011. See Also: www.great-quotes.com/cgi-bin/viewquotes.cgi?action=search&Movie=The+Lord+of+the+Rings:+The+Two+Towers.
4. Charles Spurgeon, Quoted by Richard Foster, *Finding Prayer's True Heart* (Harper-Collins: New York, NY; 1992), 179.
5. C. T. Studd, Quoted by Stephen Olford, *Not I, But Christ* (Crossway Books: Wheaton, ILL; 1995), 124.
6. Ole Hallesby, *Prayer* (Augsburg Fortress: Minneapolis, MN, 1994), 19.
7. William Law, Quoted by David G. Myers, *Psychology Through the Eyes of Faith* (Council for Christian Colleges and Universities - Harper-Collins; New York, NY; 2003), 101.
8. Bob Pierce, Quoted by Franklin Graham, *Bob Pierce: This One Thing I Do* (Nashville, TN: Thomas Nelson; 1983),156.
9. Martin H. Manser, *The Westminster Collection of Christian Quotations* (John Knox Press: Louisville, KY; 2001), 368.
10. Luther, Quoted by Wesley Duewel, *Mighty Prevailing Prayer* (Zondervan: Grand Rapids, MI, 1990), 157.
11. Ibid.
12. Oswald Chambers, Quoted by Mary Ann Bridgewater, *Prayers for the Faithful* (B & H Publishing: Nashville, TN; 2008), 205.
13. Samuel Chadwick, Quoted by Wesley Duewel, *Mighty Prevailing Prayer*, 76.

14 Ibid, 76.

Discussion Guide

1. In the story of the friend in the middle - the vagrant friend evidently feels comfortable enough to come to his friend's house at midnight. Do you think we, as Christians, maintain relationships with the hurting that invite them to come to us when they are in need? Or do we tend to cling more closely to one another?
2. The story is built to emphasize our need for persistence in prayer - do you think we give up too easily? That we pray to casually? Without passion and persistence? Why?
3. Review the elements of a good intercessor-evangelist - Do you have a relationship with people in need? Does the church have relationship with some need-sector in the city?
4. Is your church gracious to people who show up with a need? Who are different?
5. Is there a willingness to be inconvenience for the purpose of evangelism?
6. Are empathy and compassion alive in the church for the needs of people, particularly the unsaved, of the community?
7. What 'bold actions' are you taking as an individual to reach others and get them bread? What bold actions is your church taking?
8. Do you allow your heart to be broken with the things that break the heart of God?
9. Do you think your church is concerned about the conditions, the people and things that Christ would be concerned about if he were in your city?
10. William Law observed, "There is nothing that makes us love a man so much as praying for him." Agree or disagree? Who are you praying for?

All that is gold does not glitter, not all those who wander are lost; The old that is strong does not wither, Deep roots are not reached by the frost. From the ashes a fire shall be woken, A light from the shadows shall spring; Renewed shall be blade that was broken, The crownless again shall be king.[1]

CHAPTER EIGHT
THE PRAYER PRINCIPLES OF JESUS ABOUT THE MIDDLE

The next thing Jesus does in the passage in Luke is offer principles extracted from the story.

> *So I say to you, ask, and it will be given to you; seek, and you will find; knock, and it will be opened to you. For everyone who asks receives, and he who seeks finds, and to him who knocks it will be opened.*
>
> *If a son asks for bread from any father among you, will he give him a stone? Or if he asks for a fish, will he give him a serpent instead of a fish? Or if he asks for an egg, will he offer him a scorpion?*
>
> *If you then, being evil, know how to give good gifts to your children, how much more will your heavenly Father give the Holy Spirit to those who ask Him!* (Luke 11:9-13)

The Need for Persistence

"Ask" – is in the present tense. It means, "ask and *keep on* asking!" The same principle follows with the terms seek and knock. Seek and *keep-on* seeking. Knock and *keep on* knocking. Not only are these terms in the present tense, but they are also in the imperative mood. We are to ask and keep-on asking with passion, with intensity, with determination, with an I-cannot-be-denied, life-and-death disposition.

Jesus says, if we ask in this way, *"it will be given."* And if we seek persistently, *"we will find."* And further, if we knock and keep on knocking, the closed door will open. Such a privilege is not afforded to a few, but to *"everyone who asks"* with persistence and passion.

In the story, the friend with plenty was resistant. The friend in the middle, the character that represents you and I, is compassionate and accepting. The friend-with-plenty, the character who supposedly represented God, was contrary. He did not appear to have compassion. He didn't care about the hunger problem of our traveling friend. His own convenience and comfort was his main concern. This is disturbing and perplexing. Why would Jesus tell the story in this way?

The story is constructed to deliberately place the pressure on the friend-in-the middle. Will he persevere? Will he overcome the initial refusal from his affluent neighbor? Neither the benevolent nature of God, nor his capacity to meet the need is to be doubted. The friend-with-plenty, by inference God, will always have plenty and he will benevolently respond. The problem in prayer is not with God, but with us. We give up too easily.

> *If we stayed at home and did nothing, doom would find us anyway, sooner or later.*[2]

We pray once and find either creative or harmful ways to survive without God's answer. We pray, but without holy passion. The passive and passionless nature of our praying gives us away. Our lack of determination and fervor suggests that we can live without the answers that we say we seek.

Such prayers rarely move God. Samuel Chadwick once observed,

> Great grief prays with great earnestness. Prayer is not a collection of balanced phrases; it is the pouring out of the soul. What is love if it be not fiery? What are prayers if the heart be not ablaze? They are the battles of the soul. In them, men wrestle with principalities and powers...The prayer that prevails is not the work of lips and fingertips. It is the cry of a broken heart and the travail of a stricken soul.[3]

Jesus laces an important principle into the tale, *"He will not rise and give to him because he is friend."* The relationship alone is not enough. While it is strong enough to allow a visit at midnight – we can pray anytime – the relationship itself does not move the prosperous friend to meet the requested need. Prayer alone, the act of praying, is not enough. Some folks seem to think that even prayer is not required – God sees our needs, and surely he will automatically meet those needs. After all, we are his children. He loves us. Such a view is misguided. You must pray, you must ask. But that alone is not enough. You must ask with a certain level of intensity and determination. Passion is required. Jesus says, *"Because of his persistence, he will rise and give him as many as he needs."*

It is not the relationship alone that meets the need, although the request itself could not be made without it. It is because of "persistence." In the story, the relationship with the prosperous friend is intentionally tested. This is an amazing principle. Behind the passion is faith! The friend in the middle knows that the prosperous friend "can" meet the need. And he believes, that with persistence, the prosperous friend "will" meet the need.

Likewise, when we pray, faith is necessary. First, faith in the ability of God. But second, in the character of God – and beyond that, in the strength of our relationship with God. The friend in the middle had faith, that the relationship was strong enough to allow a demand! A bold request.

Jesus teaches us here that prayer is required, not suggested, but utterly essential. And further, that a certain kind of prayer emerges, based on faith in the strength of the relationship. The relationship alone is not enough. Breakthrough prayer often requires strong determination and staying power. Here is the fascinating twist. With a choice between two friends, one with plenty and one in need, one that is stable and one that is transit, one fully supplied and the other without, one with abundant bread and the other hungry, one secure and the

> FRODO: I can't do this, Sam.
>
> SAM: I know. It's all wrong. By rights we shouldn't even be here. But we are. It's like in the great stories, Mr. Frodo, the ones that really mattered, full of darkness and danger, they were. And sometimes you didn't want to know the end, because how could the end be happy? How could the world go back to the way it was when so much bad had happened? But in the end, it's only a passing thing, this shadow. Even darkness must pass. A new day will come. And when the sun shines it will shine out the clearer. Those were the stories that stayed with you. That meant something, even if you were too small to understand why. But I think, Mr. Frodo, I do understand. I know now. Folk in those stories had lots of chances of turning back, only they didn't. They kept going. Because they were holding on to something.
>
> FRODO: What are we holding onto, Sam?
>
> SAM: That there's some good in this world, Mr. Frodo... and it's worth fighting for.[4]

other vulnerable – which one would be the more important one to preserve? Most of us would lean toward preserving the relationship with the friend who has abundance. The story here urges the opposite action. It is the relationship with the one with plenty that is placed at risk here. The friend-in-the-middle is brought to a point in the story, where he seems willing to sacrifice a beneficial relationship, one that might advance to his own benefit, to meet the need in another relationship with a needy person who might never be able to repay. What a valuable host the friend-in-the-middle has become to the man in need! This is the value of intercession.

This is Abraham, on the bluff, overlooking the cities of the plain, getting into the face of the Angel of the Lord and boldly asking, *"Would you destroy the righteous with the wicked? Far be it from you to do such a thing! Shall not the judge of the earth do right?"* (Genesis 18:25). What a moment. Suddenly Abraham realizes the implications of his action and he confesses with amazement, *"I am but dust and ashes, and I have taken it upon myself to speak unto the Lord"* (Genesis 18:27). This is Moses, interceding with God, pleading for the life of the nation, after the sin of the golden calf (Deuteronomy 9).

No Mere Friend – A Caring Father

This story is troubling in one sense. It compares God to a resistant friend with plenty whose door we have to beat down to get an answer. But the story is actually not about comparison, but contrast. After telling the story, as Jesus explains it, he doesn't *compare* the friend with plenty to God the Father. Rather, he *contrasts* the friend with plenty to God. There is a difference. *"If a son asks for bread from any father among you, will he give him a stone?"*

The answer is "No!" Jesus changes the nature of the relationship of the friend-in-the-middle and the friend-with-plenty. We are no longer merely a friend asking a friend. We are sons and daughters asking our Father. Mortal men, even sinful men, do sometimes respond to the needs of others – sometimes with great pressure to do so, as in our story. "If you then, being evil, know how to give good gifts…"

If by sheer persistence, we can move an unconcerned and dispassionate friend, *"How much more will your heavenly father give?"* – What a line! *"How much more"* will God, the Father, respond to prayers from his own children. We must not give up in prayer. God is more willing to meet needs than we think he is. If mortal friends around us can be moved to meet needs – *"How much more!"* will our heavenly Father meet our needs and those of the hungry around us? Pray – and keep on praying!

There is a second contrast. Not only is God not like the friend with plenty, we are not like the friend in the middle. We don't persist in prayer. We give up too easily.

Prayer and Restoration

Prayer is the key to the restoration of all we lost in Adam's fall.

If a son shall ask bread of any of you that is a father, will he give him a stone? or if he ask a fish, will he for a fish give him a serpent? Or if he shall ask an egg, will he offer him a scorpion? (Luke 11:11-12)

These three, according to Jesus, are often the objects of our prayers – bread, fish and an egg. Suddenly, we are back to Genesis – authority over the ground and what it brings forth (bread), over the sea (fish), and over the air (bird eggs). Here is prayer's restorative role. Here is the last Adam, Jesus, the Christ, coaching us in the recovery of what was lost by the first. Each of these - the bread, the fish, the egg – has a surrogate, a deadly substitute. A stone seeks the place of bread. A serpent stands in the place of the fish. And a scorpion would take the place of the egg. What is the meaning here?

Jesus seems to be saying that prayer builds in a protection against lethal substitutes. What if Adam and Eve had paused at the tree? What if they had sought the advice of God? What if they had invited him to join them and the serpent with the deadly fruit in view? Things submitted to God by prayer invite his shielding surveillance. While the Evil One might want to trick us with "stones turned to bread," prayer protects us from deadly substitutions. The loaves of bread in the day of Jesus were round and oval in shape, much like the uncut stones of the Judean hillside. A hungry man might succumb to a mirage that caused him to see a valley full of loaves of bread, when he was only seeing stones. The Sea of Galilee had an abundance of eel-like creatures. Net fisherman had to be vigilant. When the nets were pulled up and the fish emptied into the small boats, a wreathing serpent might be found among the fish. Every fisherman was a snake handler. He quickly captured the creature and threw him overboard. Scorpions could curl up into a small ball and would sometimes hide among bird eggs. An undiscerning gatherer could think that they were picking up

> *A hungry and desperate friend may be driven into your living room because a very real tangible need. But only persistent prayer will open a cosmic door, by which God can reveal himself to that person.*

a handful of eggs only to be bitten by a venomous scorpion.

No Christian should reserve prayer for only the major things in life. Pray about everything. Invite God into every decision. Refuse to go solo. *"Without me, you can do nothing!"* Prayer invites God's provision and protection. It brings salvation and deliverance. It heightens discernment. It restores lost authority, over land, sea and air. The restoration of "all authority" is linked to prayer.

Prayer – From One Level to Another

Asking – in relation to prayer, almost always has to do with needs.

Seeking – is usually related to God Himself, specifically to His face. *"When You said, 'Seek My face,' My heart said to You, 'Your face, LORD, I will seek'"* (Psalm 27:8). The familiar 2 Chronicles 7:14 echoes the theme,

> *If My people who are called by my name will humble themselves, and pray and <u>seek my face</u>...and turn from their wicked ways, then I will hear from heaven, and will forgive their sin and heal their land.*

First Chronicles 16:11 declares, *"Seek the Lord and His strength; Seek <u>His face</u> evermore!"* To go after the *face* of God is to employ His strength! (See also: Psalm 24:6; Psalm 105:4; Hosea 5:15) Seeking is usually related to a longing for an encounter with *the face of God.* It is beyond the material, past the perishable. It is longing for the eternal person of God, Himself.

Knocking – has to do with a *doorway,* some passageway, a transition from one dimension to another. It is sin, knocking at the door that blocks Cain's blessing (Genesis 4:7). He never crossed the threshold to know the dimension on the other side of his superficial, self serving worship. It marked him for the rest of his life. It is at the threshold, sitting in the tent door, where Abraham observes the heavenly trio that will change his life forever. And it is again at the tent door, with Sarah listening from the other side, that the declaration comes that finally breaks the barrenness and allows the aging couple to move into another dimension of the promises of God (Genesis 18:1-2, 10). It is on the door posts that the redemptive blood of the Lamb is stained, and as a result, Israel is protected from the death angel in the night. All who hide behind the bloody door will live. And it is through those blood-stained doors that they pass in the night from bondage to freedom (Exodus 12:7, 22-23). It is at the door, the threshold, that a slave makes his decision to serve the house of his master forever (Exodus 21:6). At the door, the threshold, he is marked and he passes into a new relationship. It was into the doorway, at the threshold, that Elisha called the barren Shunamite woman and prophesied the birth of her child (2 Kings 4: 15). Jesus himself is the door (John 10:7, 9). John saw a door that granted revelation opened to him in heaven (Revelation 4:1). The second coming of Jesus is likened to a door – *"When you see all these things, know that it is near – at the doors!"* Matthew 24:33. That is movement to the ultimate dimension.[5]

Knocking is standing at a passageway. Something is hidden on the other side – a room, a garden, a vast arena, another dimension. We asked – and He has answered. He is real. We have sought an audience with him - and we have been introduced to him. Now, he invites us to leave one dimension and come into another, to leave the old life and enter a new.

We are often motivated to pray for "felt needs." But all the physical bread in the world can't satisfy the hunger of the soul.

That is fulfilled only in a renewed relationship with God. A hungry and desperate friend may be driven into your living room because a very real tangible need. But only persistent prayer will open a cosmic door, by which God can reveal himself to that person, in order to show them his love and life. "I'm alive," God says.

First, we pray for the person in need. But the ultimate goal is to invite the friend-in-need to pray for himself, to move him beyond merely asking for a solution to the immediate crisis. This is moving them beyond "asking" to "seeking" the face of God, until they stand at the doorway of new relational dimension, "knocking" in order to enter into a completely new sphere of living.

If I were the friend-in-need, and you, the host, went to your friend-with-plenty, and told him about my need, and he gave you bread for me, then surely I would want to meet that friend – to shake his hand and see his face. Some people demand chronic prayer, and never desire to know God. Others, will move beyond asking, and seek Him not merely for what He did for them, but for who He is. That is our goal, our hope, for our friends in need.

In the end, He will give *"the Holy Spirit to those who ask Him!"* (Luke 11:9-13). It isn't physical bread that God offers, it is Himself. Now, the man on the end, the man who had no relationship with the friend-with-plenty, has a Father! He has now moved from the end – to the middle. He is in another dimension.

Reviewing the Principles

Here are the principles:

1. We are created for the middle in Adam. And in Christ, it is again to the middle that we are now called.
2. Prayer takes place from the middle. Jesus was destined

to pray from the middle cross. There he split humanity down the middle with belief on one side and unbelief on the other. He did not merely come to the earth to die. He came to earth to die praying.

3. <u>The middle is uncomfortable, yet strategic</u>. It is inconvenient, yet essential.

4. All of us are <u>unqualified for the middle</u>. We do not have the bread necessary to give away. What is needed by our friends in need is beyond our capacity to produce. Feeling inadequate, it is tempting to move to the end, to find someone we feel is more qualified to meet the need of others in need.

4. Staying in <u>the middle requires persistence</u>. We must ask – and keep on asking, seek – and keep on seeking, knock – and keep on knocking. The whole story is built to emphasize the need for determination, for tenacity. In verse 11, the metaphor changes. Jesus now suggests that we are not seeking bread from a friend, but we are like a son seeking bread from a father.

5. <u>There is a protection in prayer</u>. Asking for bread, we will not get a stone. .... Somehow when we submit an issue to God in prayer, he promises a protection over subtle and deadly substitutions. What should we pray about? Everything!

6. He gives the Holy Spirit to those who ask! If the person on the end, without a relationship with the friend with plenty, without a father-son connection, now has the Holy Spirit, what has taken place? The impartation of the Spirit implies son-ship! <u>The friend in need,</u> the friend on the end, <u>has now moved to the middle</u>.

1. Tolkien, *The Lord of the Rings, The Followship of the Ring,* 193. In the film version, Arwen is given these lines. In the original print version, they come from a poem by the character, Bilbo.
2. Tolkien, *The Lord of the Rings: Return of the King,* Chapter 4.
3. www.epm.org/artman2/publish/prayer/*Great_Quotes_On_Prayer*.shtml
4. Tolkien, *The Lord of the Rings, The Two Towers.*
5. See: *Entertaining God and Influencing Cities* (Alive Publications: Kannapolis, NC; 2009), for a complete chapter on the Threshold Covenant.

Discussion Guide

1. Why is it important that "asking" is in the imperative mood and the present tense? What does that imply about your praying?

2. Do you think our lack of passion and persistence – our mood and mode of prayer is what God sees as real prayer, as opposed to our words. We 'say' we must have revival, but we do it without tears. What does God see as prayer? Our talk or our tears or lack of tears?

3. In the parable, the relationship is not enough. Prayer is not enough. Persistent prayer is required. Why?

4. When you have to choose between two friends – or even two different 'classes' of people to please, who do prefer? The poor or the powerful. The down-and-out powerless or the affluent and influential? Does your church cater to one class and kind of people? If the needy and hungry knocked on your door, would they be welcome?

5. In the interpretation of the parable, it is clear that God is not being compared to the friend with plenty, but contrasted with him. Talk about what that means.

6. Discuss the 'how much more' of the passage. How do we get to that 'how much more?'

7. How is prayer the key to the restoration of what we lost in Adam's fall?

8. Review the principles in the chapter.

9. Do you now have a better understanding of the critical, uncomfortable middle?

10. What middle is God calling you to?

Over the land there lies a long shadow. The tower tembles; to the tombs of kings. The Dead awaken; for the hour is come for the oath breakers: at the Stone of Erech they shall stand again and hear there a horn in the hills ringning. Whose shall be the horn? Who shall call them from the gray twilight, the forgotten people? The heir of him to whom the oath they swore. He shall pass the Door to the Paths of the Dead.[1]

Eowyn: Then she stared at him as one that is sticken, and her face blanched, and for long she spoke no more, while all sat silent. *"But, Aragon, is it then your errand to seek death? For that is all you will find on that road. They do not suffer the living to pass."*

Aragorn: *"They may suffer me to pass. No other road will serve."*

Eowyn: *"But this is madness."*

Aragon: *"It is not madness, lady, for I go on a path appointed… because I must. Only so can I see any hope of doing my part in the war against Sauron."* [2]

Lights went out in house and hamlet as they came, and doors were shut, and folk that were afield cried in terror and ran wild like hunted deer. *"The King of the Dead! The King of the Dead is come upon us!"* Bells were ringing far below. Elrohir gave Aragorn a silver horn, and he blew upon it and there was the sound of answering horns. A great host gathered all about the hill. Aragorn dismounted. Standing by the Stone, he cried in a great voice: *"Oathbreakers, why have you come?"* Out of the darkness a voice was heard. *"To fulfill our oath and have peace."*

Aragorn: *"The hour is come at last. And when the land is clean of the servants of Sauron, I will hold the oath fulfilled, and you shall have peace and depart for ever. For I am Elessar, Isildur's heir of Gondor."*

And with that, he bade the great standard unfurled. There was silence. Not a whisper. Not a sigh. When dawn came, he led the company forth. No other mortal Men could have endured it.[3]

CHAPTER NINE
LIBERATING THE FALLEN HOUSE OF ADAM

And he was casting out a devil, and it was dumb [mute]. And it came to pass, when the devil was gone out, the dumb [mute] spake; and the people wondered.

But some of them said, He casteth out devils through Beelzebub the chief of the devils. And others, tempting him, sought of him a sign from heaven. But he, knowing their thoughts, said unto them, Every kingdom divided against itself is brought to desolation; and a house divided against a house falleth.

If Satan also be divided against himself, how shall his kingdom stand? because ye say that I cast out devils through Beelzebub. And if I by Beelzebub cast out devils, by whom do your sons cast them out? therefore shall they be your judges. But if I with the finger of God cast out devils, no doubt the kingdom of God is come upon you.

When a strong man armed keepeth his palace, his goods are in peace: But when a stronger than he shall come upon him, and overcome him, he taketh from him all his armour wherein he trusted, and divideth his spoils. He that is not with me is against me: and he that gathereth not with me scattereth.

When the unclean spirit is gone out of a man, he walketh through dry places, seeking rest; and finding none, he saith, I will return unto my house whence I came out. And when he cometh, he findeth it swept and garnished. Then goeth he, and taketh to him seven other spirits more wicked than himself; and they enter in, and dwell there: and the last state of that man is worse than the first.

> *Adam is not only an individual...but a corporate mass of humanity...the federal head of the fallen human race. He is our flesh-father. We all have his flawed DNA. He died not as the free man he was created to be, with dominion. Rather, he died in captivity, a prisoner in his own fallen house. Satan illegitimately seized control of Adam's house and his kingly scepter, and continues to hold all born into it hostage to death by sin.*

And it came to pass, as he spake these things, a certain woman of the company lifted up her voice, and said unto him, Blessed is the womb that bare thee, and the paps which thou hast sucked. But he said, Yea rather, blessed are they that hear the word of God, and keep it (Luke 11:14-28, KJV).

Dietrich Bonhoeffer was a German pastor in the 1930's. He had a front row seat during the transformation of Germany and the rise of Hitler. Sadly, most church leaders welcomed Nazism. They were on Hitler's bandwagon, his supporters. Bonhoeffer was one of the few opposing voices. His peers had succumbed to a model of faith that could fit into the radical revolutionary Nazi mindset. They had adapted a culturally conditioned and politically correct Christianity. They never saw the train-wreck coming. For Bonhoeffer, the problem was not merely a political or social issue, not simply one of cultural conformity and adaptation, it was spiritual. "We must decide, we must discern between the spirits," he argued. A spirit was sweeping through Germany and it was about to rattle the globe. An unholy anointing was loose in the land and few discerned it.

We are now watching a similar dynamic play out in America. Few people are aware of the historic and symbiotic connections between Islam and Nazism. They were both fervent in their desire for global domination, their hatred of Jews, and the desire to eradicate or alter genuine Christian faith. And they collaborated during World War 2. Both have violent cultic roots.[4]

Bonhoeffer conducted a veritable one man crusade against the evil. He would sometimes give an address, beginning his talk to a room full of people, only to end his presentation with a nearly empty room. Like Israel in the

> *We have detonated a nuclear device that has made the whole planet radioactive in a spiritual sense – and everyone has cancer as a result. We and our offspring are deformed, in heart and soul. We reject such a notion only because the human template is now so radically warped that we no longer recongnize normal.*

days of Jeremiah, his German peers did not want to hear the truth, so they walked out! Near the end of the war, he confronted his fellow churchmen, calling for a public confession of their guilt, their failure to be a moral voice of constraint in the face of evil. It was clear at that point, that Hitler's reign was not yielding the promises his charismatic speeches had envisioned. Germany was living a nightmare. Would his fellow churchmen come out from the shadows and stand like prophets calling the nation back to moral sanity? He lamented, "The church was silent where it had to cry out...It had witnessed the lawless application of brutal force, the physical and spiritual suffering of countless innocent people, opposition, hatred and murder, and...it had not raised its voice on behalf of the victims and has not found a way to hasten to their aid. It is guilty of the death of the weakest and most defenseless brothers of Jesus Christ."[5] But no one joined the theologian in his lament. No one emerged boldly from the shadows to challenge the crumbling Third Reich. And for his virtually lone voice, he would die as a martyr. Bonhoeffer would say:

> The great masquerade of evil has played havoc with all our ethical concepts. For evil to appear disguised as light, charity, historical necessity, or social justice is quite bewildering to anyone brought up on our traditional ethical concepts...Who stands fast? Only the person whose final standard is not his reason, principles, conscience, freedom, or virtue, but who is ready to sacrifice all this when called to obedient and responsible action in faith and in exclusive allegiance to God – the responsible person, who tries to make his whole life an answer to the question and call of God.[6]

Now, we may be standing on the brink of the rise of another dark kingdom – the ultimate anti-Christian regime. Will the church continue its political correctness? Will it dare to differentiate itself from culture and be a prophetic voice? Will it step to

> But to the Riders of the Mark it seems so long ago, that the raising of this house is but a memory of song, and the years before are lost in the mist of time. Now they call this land their home, their own, and their speech is sundered from their northern kin'. Then he began to chant softly in a slow tongue unknown to the Elf and Dwarf; yet they listened, for there was a strong music in it...I cannot guess what it means...it is laden with the sadness of Mortal Men. Where now are the horse and the rider? Where is the horn that was blowing? The bright hair flowing? The hand on the harpstring, and the red fire glowing? Where is the spring and the harvest and the tall corn growing? They have passed like rain on the mountain, like a wind in the meadow; The days have gone down in the West behind the hills into shadow.[7]

the middle? Will it deal with its own moral compromise, its own lukewarm condition?

Why Man Was Created

Luke 11:14-28, is a graduate course in prayer and the uncomfortable middle. Man was created unique from all creation. God, breathed into him. God deposited a bit of Himself in man. Adam was fashioned to be a duplex. Inside the body God generously and completely gave him was a special dwelling place for God. Man was formed to be a clay temple, his heart, a host to God. Of all the places God could have chosen as a dwelling place in the earth, he chose not a special spot in nature, but a place in the center of man. Adam was a combination of heaven and earth. He was made from the dust of the earth itself, to resemble the animal kingdom over which he had dominion. And yet, he was also made to reflect the image of God for whom he exercised that dominion and from whom that dominion was given.

Evolutionary science has done a great disservice to man. It has made him a product of chance, a mere extension of the animal kingdom, an evolved mass of particles with amazing DNA complexity. In the end, evolution has made man a graduated beast in a beastly world. And the current generation believes the lie. In truth, man was more like God than the world in which he was placed. He was not a physical creature with a spiritual dimension. He was a spiritual creature with a physical compliment.

Indeed, modern science should renounce Darwinism and admit its error in view of the stunning discoveries in recent years. Present-day genetic discoveries are astounding. The simple cell, with the discovery of the double helix that comprises the DNA found in every cellular structure in the human body, cannot be called 'simple' anymore. The amount of data in each cell, once decoded, equals a multi-volume set of encyclopedias.

Holding it all together, indeed, binding the cellular structure and therefore the body together is yet another astounding discovery – laminins. This family of proteins are the integral structural scaffolding of the basement membranes in our tissue. They are cell adhesion molecules. Without them, we would fall apart. What is more amazing is that laminins are large trimeric proteins containing an α-chain, a β-chain and a γ-chain, found in five, three and three genetic variants, respectively. These trimeric proteins form a cross – that's right – a cross! At the center of every cell in the human body is a cross.[8] Maybe that's why the Holy Spirit declared through Paul, *"All things were created through Him and for Him. And He is before all things, and in Him all things consist"* (Colossians 1:15-17). The term *consist* means all things "are held together."

Man was made a noble creation – with a slice of God in his heart. While nature bears the fingerprints of God, man bore his image. And this is not mere poetic language. Man was created for the middle. He was designed to stand between creation and the Creator, between earth and heaven. He was the mediator. The distance between the noble creature man and that of the angels was but "a little" according to Psalm 8. Man is more kin to angels than apes. But man fell. And he fell a much further distance than we realize. He fell far enough, that emerging from the fall, he felt, thought and postured more closely with creation than the Creator. He was more aligned with beasts and birds, the visible, than with the Invisible Designer. He could see in himself – all forms of created beings. He had more difficulty seeing in himself the invisible God.

The disconnect is real. The size of the gap is stunning. The implications of the fall are disastrous. No human can close the gap. No man can climb to heaven. No one is qualified to broker peace between heaven and earth. None here recognize the degree to which our sin is offensive to heaven. But it is more than merely offensive. We have detonated a nuclear device that has made the whole planet radioactive in a spiritual sense – and everyone has cancer as a result. We and our offspring are deformed, in heart and soul. We reject such a notion only because the human template is now so radically warped that we no longer recognize normal. We now live in a spiritually and morally toxic climate. Sin is not merely an idea. Sin is real, and its effects are deadly. It infects the atmosphere. It pollutes the environment. It cannot be merely "forgiven" and be expected to disappear. It has a lasting impact. What is to be done with the toxic waste created by sin? Like nuclear waste, it is real, and who wants the deadly residue in their refrigerator or their backyard? Something had to be done to restore the planet, to rid the planet of the lethal toxins. Sin is the ultimate environmental hazard – the one spoken of by no green advocate. The Old Testament points out the connection. Sin defiles the land. The planet itself and its atmosphere is poisoned by sin (Numbers 35:33).[9]

The natural laws that govern the universe are parallel to spir-

Intercession – The Uncomfortable Strategic Middle

> *Three rings for the Elven-kings under the sky, Seven for the Dwarf-lords in their halls of stone. Nine for Mortal Men doomed to die, One for the Dark Lord on his dark throne. In the Land of Mordor where the Shadows lie.*[10] *One Ring to find them. One Ring to bring them all and in the darkness bind them. In the Land of Mordor where the Shadows lie. This is the Master-ring, the One Ring to rule them all. This is the One Ring that he lost many ages ago, to the great weakening of his power. He greatly desires it – but he must not get it. Frodo sat silent and motionless. Fear seemed to stretch out a fast hand, like a dark cloud rising in the East and looming up to engulf him. "This ring," he stammered. "How, how on earth did it come to me?"*[11]

itual laws. In an environment of rogue and rebellious thinking, some assert that God can do anything he wants to do. He could merely summon His Angels and fix the broken world. It is not true. The spiritual and moral laws that govern our physical world are extensions of the essence of God Himself. Were He to violate those laws, He would be at war with Himself, and He would do harm and wrong to Himself. It is impossible for God to violate truth or lie! (Hebrews 6:18). It is impossible for Him to respond to a temptation to do some wrong or commit an evil (James 1:13). The game of life cannot be rigged – it must be played by the rules, consequences and all. He cannot and will not act in contradiction to His nature. He is authentically true to Himself. There is no hypocrisy, no duplicity in Him. He is true and faithful (Revelation 19:11). The entire universe is governed by these moral laws of God. He is the universal Judge. Any violation of God's moral or relational order must be appropriately adjudicated in His divine court. God gave – really and genuinely gave – the rights of authority and dominion over the earth to man. "It was a bona fide gift!" as Billheimer argues.[12] Man was not given *the earth*, *"The earth is the Lord's!"* (Psalm 24:1) But he was given authority *over the earth*, a stewardship trust – and he lost it to Satan. If God had chosen in that moment to become a crooked judge, to change the rules, to void the fall, to ignore reality, He would have violated truth. He had to play by his own rules. He had to act consistent with his own character. He was honest – even in his dealings with Lucifer. Legally lost, the earth had

> **GANDALF:** He's suffered a defeat, yes, but... behind the walls of Mordor, our enemy is regrouping.
>
> **GIMLI:** Let him stay there. Let him rot! Why should we care?
>
> **GANDALF:** Because ten-thousand Orcs now stand between Frodo and Mount Doom. I've sent him to his death.
>
> **ARAGORN:** No. There is still hope for Frodo. He needs time... and safe passage across the plains of Gorgoroth. We can give him that.
>
> **GIMLI:** How?
>
> **ARAGORN:** Draw out Sauron's armies...Gather our full strength and march on the Black Gate. We can give Frodo his chance if we keep Sauron's Eye fixed upon us. Keep him blind to all else that moves.
>
> **LEGOLAS:** A diversion.
>
> **GIMLI:** Certainty of death, small chance of success... What are we waiting for?[14]

to be legally redeemed. There could be no fault on the part of God, no accusation that would not pass the test of truth and fairness. Because the legal rights had belonged to man, only a man could redeem the earth. That is why no angel could have been sent. That is why, from a logical and legal point of view, the incarnation is not a side-bar doctrine, not an optional concept. And, if the last Adam, had failed to be moral and had fallen as the first Adam had, there would have been no hope for humanity. The rules had to be observed.[13] The only treatment for sin and death is at the foot of the cross.

Why Jesus Came

The thesis of this little book has been that Jesus came to bring salvation and to re-secure the intercessory middle that had been surrendered in Adam's fall. Mankind, consisting of the sons and daughters of Adam, were helpless after the fall. They could neither defend themselves nor throw off the tyranny of Satan's illegitimate rule. The earth was not and is not the property of the Evil One. On the Mount of Temptation, though Satan dared, in the face of Christ himself, to claim that the kingdoms of this world were his to give (Matthew 4:1-11), he was and is a liar (John 8:44). *"The earth is the Lords, and the fullness thereof"* (Psalm 24:1; 1 Corinthians 10:26). He created it. And Christ was instrumental in that creation (Colossians 1:16). And having given it as a gift to man (Genesis 1:28), only to have man indiscriminately give its rights away by sin, the Creator became, in Christ, the Redeemer (Galatians 3:13-14; 1 Pet. 1:18). He bought it back again – with blood (Revelation 5:9). The earth and its inhabitants are therefore, twice His. And yet, despite the virgin birth and sinless life of Christ, both of which differentiated Jesus from Adam, fused with the resurrection and ascension, the enthronement of Christ and the empowerment of the Church by the Holy Spirit's anointing, the Evil One refuses to relent.

Jesus came to displace him, to destroy him and all his works (1 John 3:8). The Greek for *cast out* in this passage is *ekballo*, a powerful word, which means to cast forth, drive out, or expel. *Ballo* means to eject - literally or figuratively. It can mean to thrust, send away or send out. Jesus wants to eject Lucifer from the earth – to banish him.

Any discussion of the middle is incomplete without visiting this point. Jesus, the Christ, the Lord of the earth (Matthew 28:18; Ephesians 1:20-22; 1 Corinthians 15:24), now occupies the premier role of intercession in heaven (Romans 8:34; Hebrews 7:25). He stands as an advocate for mankind before the Father. He represents us in heaven's courtroom. He has a right to do so. He was born of woman and was tempted as a man, yet overcame (Galatians 4:4-5; Hebrews 4:15). His sinless and innocent death demands justice. We, rebel earthlings, killed God. This was Peter's message at Pentecost. God had come in Christ, and sinful men had killed him (Acts 2:22-23, 36). What is the penalty for the murder of a king? It is and was an act of war. And yet, the dying plea of Jesus was, *"Father, forgive them!"* (Luke 23:34) Did that prayer cancel out all retribution for the unthinkable assassination of the Messiah, the King of the earth? (2 Thessalonians 1:8; Revelation 6:1; 19:2; Jude 15; John 5:27) No, but it has created a window of grace in which the Holy Spirit works through the Church, the bride partner of Jesus, to enable us to stand as intercessors in the earth (Romans 8:26). In our union with Christ, by the Spirit, we contest the illegitimate reign of Lucifer over the souls of men, and we seek to bring light into this dark world, to wake up its inhabitants from the night-sleep, the spell that they are under by the power of sin and death (Isaiah. 51:9; 52:1; 2 Corinthians 4:4).

The bride-partner role of the redeemed is underemphasized, and the result is a passive church. It is the "Spirit and the bride" together who are to say, *"Come!"* to the wedding feast (Revelation 22:17). The great need is for the church to be mobilized, to align herself with the will and purposes of God, to became a forceful agent for the Spirit. As the church travails, empathetically praying for the lost world, for lost sons and daughter, the Spirit convicts and convinces, opens eyes and softens hearts, woos resistant men and women into a love relationship with Jesus Christ. The Church prays by the Spirit, and the Spirit works in partnership with the Church. No praying – no drawing by the Spirit. No travail – no wooing of the lost by the Spirit. The two work together.

The middle to which Christ came was not empty. As we have noted previously, it was illegitimately occupied. And despite the triumph of the Crucified, it is still illegally occupied. Jesus came specifically to re-secure the middle, to defeat the dark powers, and to create a bridge by which mankind could access the only true and living God through the cross. And he has done that - physically and spiritually, and with finality, and yet, the middle is still contested. Though the bridge to God, the Father is present, many are bound and cannot cross it. Two billion do not know that it even exists. And demonic forces still attempt to block the bridge. They hinder the work of evangelism, blind the hearts of men, and engage in guerilla warfare

> *We want prayer to be a quick prophetic declaration - a shout at the enemy who obediently cowers. It is more like a military campaign in guerilla warfare fashion. There is no clear line of attack. Uncertainty and unsettling upsurges come from unexpected quarters. We might prefer a boxing match with the possibility of a supernatural knockout punch, but the encounter is more like "wrestling"...*

against bridge agents. So the middle is still illegitimately occupied. It seems that some part of the final triumph over the powers of darkness is left as a task for us, the bride partner (Hebrews 2:7-10; Ephesians 1:18-23; 1 Corinthians 15:25-27; Hebrews 10:12-14).

The victory is certain, despite the continued resistance. The sting of death is gone (1 Corinthians 15:55-56). The tyranny of sin's penalty is no more. After the cross and the empty tomb, Satan stands before the weakest believer, disarmed. Jesus, by his resurrection and ascension, by his enthronement and the sending of the Spirit, has rendered him powerless – defenseless and without armor. The blood defeats him. The testimony of the redeemed overcomes him. Praise overwhelms him. The presence of God crushes him. Peace bruises him under its feet. The name of Jesus shackles him. The Word of God routs him. Faith thrashes him. He is defenseless. He may growl and seek to intimidate, but his only weapons are deception and accusation (Rev. 12:9-10). Grace has triumphed (Romans 5:21; 6:14). Love has decreed an unending relationship. Yet, the enemy is still on his feet, but he is staggering. He is wounded. Even in his last ascent, John saw one of his heads wounded as to death (Revelation 13:3). His earthly reign of terror is over before it begins. His Anti-Christian global party is a light that will only flicker for a brief moment. He is finished, because salvation, and the triumph of the crucified, is finished. And yet, he continues to operate, as if he there was no virgin birth, no Christ of history, no resurrection. He, more than any human on earth, knows that Jesus is alive, seated on the throne in heaven (James 2:19). But he will not relent. He will not surrender. He will not acknowledge the restored authority of the last Adam. Lucifer continues to illegitimately occupy the middle, working as he does from the middle heaven, above the planet. He is the prince and power of the air (Ephesians 2:1-3; Daniel 10:13-20). And he has ground contacts as well, partnered with him, some willingly, some unwillingly, some unwittingly (Mark 5:2f; Acts 16:16f).

When Jesus, the Christ, stepped into the middle, first modeling the middle from the earth, as a servant-king, as a prophetic voice and a priestly-shepherd, he met Satan in the wilderness (Matthew 4). He did not fall to temptation as did the first Adam. He did not succumb to the deception. He did not bite the apple. Satan left that encounter frustrated, and defeated. But, that was only the first round. And yet, that first round set the pace for the battle between of Satan against Jesus over the next three-and-a-half years. For the first time in human history, Satan had met a man, a mortal, an individual, a human, who had the capacity and the will to say, "No!" to his deceptive ploys.

In those next few years, Jesus began the process of displacing the powers, the challenge we are now called to complete (Mark 16:17f). He disarmed the powers, one soul at a time. On the cross, he would wage his final earthly campaign by yielding to death itself! (John 12:31-32) He, in one moment, would gather up the sins of mankind and take them to hell, so no repentant human would ever have to go. Then he would enter Abraham's bosom, and liberate the Old Testament saints (1 Pet. 3:19; Ephesians 4:8).

Ascending into heaven, he would request that the Father send forth the Spirit to empower his bride-partner, the Church (John 14:16). He now calls us to continue the process of breaking ground contacts with the middle heaven, by the salvation of souls, one man and woman at a time! We are in the bloody and strategic middle. We are the body of Christ – his hands and feet, his voice and his heart extended. We represent Jesus, the head of the Church (Ephesians 1:22; 5:23). And we now stand in contrast to the body of Adam, from which we were transferred. This is the old man, the corporate mass of dying humanity (Colossians 3:9; Ephesians 4:22). It is energized by the unholy spirit of the Evil One (Ephesians 2:1-2). He too will send forth his messiah at the end of time, the Anti-Christ (1 John 4:3; 2:22; 2 Thessalonians 2:3) . He will send forth his unholy spirit, personified in the person of the false prophet (Revelation 16:13). These two incarnations with his earthly partners will be his last ditch stand to prevent Christ from claiming the planet. But the plan is doomed to fail. In the end, he will be bound by a mere angel, and cast into the bottomless pit (Revelation 20:1-2). And Christ will rule on the earth with his bride partner, the Church (2 Timothy 2:12).

Two Corporate Men – Adam and Christ

There are two corporate men on the earth! (Romans 5:12; 1 Corinthians 15:22) Every human, but one, is identified with the first of these two – Adam (Matthew 22:42-46). We are all born into Adam. All but Jesus. We inherited his fallen nature (Psalm 51:5) and became subjects (Romans 6:6; 7:14), born into a house under siege. We were not born with a choice. We were born without one. Like the children of slaves, we were born in bondage. In bondage to sin and to death, and trapped in Adam's house. The nature of the bondage was and is so clever, so ingenious, that we have the illusion of being free. We are drugged. We are deluded.

Jesus did not come to give men a choice. He came because men had no choice. Because he came, now we have a decision we must make. *"God,"* Paul says, *"by sending his own Son in the likeness of sinful man to be a sin offering...condemned sin in sinful man"* (Romans 8:3). The action of Christ at the cross – of embracing death without sin, without reviling, in complete obedience to the demands of the Old Testament moral code – met the "righteous requirements of the law". Here was a man, the first in history, who set a new stan-

> *The nexus of control is in the power of the one – "by one man."*

dard in behalf of those who would choose to *"not live according to their sinful nature but according to the Spirit"* (Romans 8:2-4). That is the desire of God for all men. The Father, through the Spirit, on the basis of the work of Christ, is drawing men to Himself. *"But I, when I am lifted up from the earth, will draw all men to myself"* (John 12:32). We can now escape (Luke 3:7; Colossians 3:6) from the body of Adam, from both its bondage to sin and sin's end - death. We can be free from the tyranny of Satan and the judgment coming on his kingdom (1 John 3:8). That requires a transfer, by repentance and the new birth, from the body of Adam, into the body of Christ. And that, requires our death (Mark 8:34; Matthew 16:24).

No one gets out of the body of Adam without dying. You must lose your life to find it (Matthew 10:39). In Adam, all die (1 Corinthians 15:22). So, we experience death, by the metaphor of baptism (1 Corinthians 12:13). Buried with Christ in baptism, identifying with his death, with his sinless life, with his utter and absolute commitment to do the will of the Father, to live a life of perfect obedience, we are raised to new life. Dead, to sin and this world, we nevertheless retain our earthly life and existence. God could in the moment of salvation take us to heaven. But He leaves us here to borrow our bodies. To make of them living, mobile temples from which He operates (Romans 8:10; 12:1-2; 1 Corinthians 12:27). We are still alive - and yet, we count ourselves as dead (Romans 6:11). We still have possessions, but we count all of them as naught for Christ, and his cause. We join the counter-revolution. It is a heart revolution, not a political one. It is a triumph by servant-hood. It is a gentle revolution of grace and forgiveness, bound to uncompromising truth. If you are a genuine believer, you are dead, in Christ. You have already had a funeral in a watery grave (Romans 6:4; Colossians 2:12). You are alive now for a different reason. You are alive to further the cause and message of

Christ. You have been left as an undercover operative in Adam's house, and you are whispering at the edges of the darkness the wonderful truth, that Jesus is not dead, but alive. You are a living witness, proof, by your faith and life, that indeed, Jesus is truly alive (Acts 1:8; 2:12, 22-24). You are now of the house of Jesus – the Christ, Lord of the Church. His resurrection is no myth. He is alive – really and truly. And he is coming back, literally, any day now, to completely liberate Adam's house (Romans 9:27-28). He has prepared a 'place' for those who believe, a permanent, eternal house (John 14:1-2).

Adam, you see, is not only an individual who lived at the dawn of creation. Adam is a corporate mass of humanity. He is the federal head of the fallen human race. He is our flesh-father. We all have his flawed DNA. Sadly, he did not die as the free man. He had been created free, with dominion over all the earth and everything in it. Sadly, he died in captivity, a prisoner in his own house, the fallen house of Adam (mankind), and with his fall, the race of humanity fell with him. Satan, who illegitimately seized control of Adam's house and his kingly scepter, continues to hold the house and all born into it hostage. Every human but one, was born into this house as a son or daughter of Adam. It is that 'One' who makes all the difference in the world. Into this world, this earth, the house of Adam, under the illegal rule of the king of darkness, came Jesus. He was born of woman, as a 'trojan' baby, from the line of King David – born to claim the throne, and to begin a quiet revolution that would end the siege of Satan over the house of Adam.

Jesus, too, is not only a real person who lived 2,000 years ago. Like Adam, he is the head of a new race of men. He is the federal head of the redeemed, the body of Christ (Revelation 3:14; Colossians 1:18; Ephesians 1:22; 5:23). By his death and burial, his resurrection, ascension and enthronement in heaven, he has forged a mystical union with believers, a new corporate mass of humanity. He is our Savior. He has come to reconnect us with our heavenly Father. By salvation, he liberates us individually, both from the penalty and the power of sin. Through his assassination, he entered death's chamber, and liberated those who had been captive to death, by sin. He paid the ransom and he led captivity captive. He now has the righteous of the Old Testament in his possession, under his control, in heaven itself. And their presence, there in heaven, is proof of the power and efficacy of his death and resurrection. For, if the power of his sinless life was sweeping enough to liberate those who died under the law, with only a promise, then how much more will it liberate those who die in the Spirit, with the fulfillment of the death, burial, resurrection, ascension and enthronement behind them?

Despite the high levels of individualism and pride in our current world, no one stands alone. We are all part of one of these two systems – the body of Adam or the body of Christ. Each has a head – one, Adam, is dead; and the other, Christ, is alive. The body of Adam appears to be alive, but it is dying. It is energized by the demonic (Ephesians 2:2). The body of Christ is energized by the Holy Spirit. Adam, and all who depend only on him for life, is dying. Christ, and all those who depend on him, are being made alive (Acts 17:28). The body of Adam is under judgment. The body of Christ has been liberated from judgment through the death of Christ. Those in Adam will face the Great White Throne Judgment (Revelation 20:11f). Those in Christ will face the judgment seat of Christ (2 Corinthians 5:10; Romans 14:10) – and that is all the difference for eternity. Those in the body of Adam, do what they please, within limits. They are actually under the power of sin and Satan. Those in the body of Christ, do the will of God. They are to be led by the Spirit. Which body are you in? Adam or Christ?

Liberating Adam's House – One Person at a Time

Jesus came to liberate those in the body of Adam. He came to liberate Adam's house. This happens simultaneously at both a micro and macro level. Luke records that:

> *Jesus was driving out a demon that was mute. When the demon left, the man who had been mute spoke, and the crowd was amazed. But some of them said, 'By Beelzebub, the prince of demons, he is driving out demons.' Others tested him by asking for a sign from heaven.* (NIV)

The word here is *daimonion*, not devil, but demon. It means *an evil spirit* or a *demon*. So a demon is a spirit, formerly an angel, now disembodied as a result of past judgment. These are fallen heavenly beings who conspired with Lucifer in his rebellion and the siege of the earth. With Lucifer, they hold Adam's children hostage.

In this passage, one individual is held captive by one of these demonic spirits. He is not only a prisoner in Adam's house, he is also a prisoner in his own body. The word for mute is *kóphos*, which actually means *deaf* – so hearing and speaking are meant here in connection one with another. The word can also mean *blunt or dull* referring to the social impact of the person's disability. The demon is characterized here as being mute."[15] It is doubtful that the demon was mute due to some incapacity. Rather, he chose to be mute – and his decision affected the condition of the man. *"When the demon left, the man...spoke."* The evil spirit had gagged the individual; muted him. Matthew adds that he was also blind (Matthew 12:22).

This is a powerful picture. A tactic of Satan and his co-conspirators is to silence the victims of his siege. The person is not, all things being normal, physically incapable of speaking or seeing. He has been spiritually immobilized, held hostage in silence and darkness. When he finally does speak, having been liberated, the crowd is amazed. He is not so much healed, in a physical sense, as he is unshackled and released from the dominating power that repressed him. Now free, he speaks. His faculties and capacities are liberated with the demon's departure. He is free! Under bondage, he could not even speak or see. Now, he must choose how he will use his freedom. Will he attempt to stay neutral - joining neither the kingdom of darkness nor the kingdom of light?

The impact of Lucifer's hold on an individual, via his demonic comrades, is varied. Some, cry out! They are used by the controlling demon to *sound forth*. Others are silenced. Both conditions are evidence of control. The Holy Spirit exercises no such debilitating control over those in whose heart he dwells. The Son has come to set us free, and we are to be free indeed!

Liberating Adam's House – the Macro Principle

The liberation of the man brings confusion and a protest by religious leaders. *"By Beelzebub, the prince of demons, he [Jesus] is driving out demons."* The older versions say *devils* but the better translation is *demons*. There is one *Devil*. There are many *demons*. The Devil is one and the same with Lucifer (Isaiah 14:11), Satan, the Dragon (Revelation 20:2; 12:9), the Tempter (Matthew 4:10), and probably Beelzebub, though some identify Beelzebub as a high ranking demon partner of Lucifer.

Here, in the accusation against Jesus, is the introduction of the macro principle. The individual man possessed by a spirit, a demonic spirit, and liberated is the micro. The larger question is, "Who controls the spirit (the demon) that controlled the demonized man?" This is a quest for the master of demons. The Pharisees alleged that it was Beelzebub, and that Jesus was his partner. The accusation is that the exorcism of Jesus was a trick. The demon left, ostensibly, since Jesus was exercising the power of the prince of demons, that he performed exorcisms by the power of Satan – acting as an agent of Beelzebub. His power, they charged, was derived from dark energy. Notice his response. Jesus knew their thoughts and said to them:

> *Any kingdom divided against itself will be ruined, and a house divided against itself will fall. If Satan is divided against himself, how can his kingdom stand? I say this because you claim that I drive out demons by Beelzebub* (Luke 11:17-18).

The *macro* shifts the focus. It is no longer on either the individual man or the individual demon. In the liberation of individual men or women from the power of any specific demon, the greater questions is, whose authority is exercised and whose authority is challenged? Jesus answers that question by introducing two related ideas – that of a *kingdom* and a *house*. "*Any <u>kingdom</u> divided against itself will be ruined, and a <u>house</u> divided against itself will fall.*" With these two images, the purpose and mission of his authority is explained.

The *kingdom* he has come to oppose is *the kingdom of Satan*, of Beelzebub, the 'master' of the demonic; and the kingdom he has come to represent, is the kingdom of heaven. The *house* he has come to liberate is not Satan's house, it is *Adam's house*. The *kingdom* of Satan has invaded and subdued Adam's house, and it has brought Adam's family and all of his descendents under a legal siege. It is legal because of Adam's sin and forfeiture of his dominion. Jesus is neither of Satan's kingdom nor of Adam's house. No one in or of Adam's house could liberate the house and throw off the dreadful tyranny of sin and Satan. If that were possible, we would need no Redeemer, no Messiah – since one from among us would be both able and qualified to be the liberating king. But earth had no such qualified or capable liberator. So Jesus came as the liberator of men (the sons of Adam) and the earth (Adam's house) itself.

The release of the sons and daughters of Adam from the tentacles of demons is not, as the Pharisee's suggest, by Satan's power, it is the *finger of God*. Jesus is not of Satan, and more surprisingly, as noted, he is not a son of Adam. He has come to bring a sword to Adam's house, which may mean father against son, and brother against brother, and mother against daughter (Mark 13:12; Matthew 10:21). He has come to liberate those who will be liberated from the tyranny of being born into the house (family) of Adam, and under the penalty of sin. Yet, his warfare is not *against* Adam's house, but in *behalf* of Adam's house and his enslaved sons. Jesus uses a specific phrase that has Old Testament roots, *"But if I with the finger of God cast out devils, no doubt the kingdom of God is come upon you"* (Luke 11:20, Exodus 8:19).

When Moses came to Pharaoh and demanded the liberation of Israel from Egypt, their freedom from slavery, Pharaoh resisted. What followed was a contest in the form of a series of plagues. Every plague - blood, frogs, flies, darkness, locust and more – was an act of war against one or more of the Egyptian gods. At first, the magicians appeared to be able to duplicate the plagues. This meant, by that standard, that Moses was no more than another run-of-the-mill *shaman*. But then, the plagues intensified in their scope. And the Egyptian magic men were not able to duplicate the plagues or reverse them. That placed Moses in a class by himself. And it also meant that the Egyptian deities were no match for Yahweh, the God of the Hebrews.

It is here that the Egyptian magicians used the phrase *"the finger of God!"* (Exodus 8:19) They recognized a divine power at work, more than human, more than that of a typical *shaman*, one they could neither channel nor combat. Pharaoh had no alternative but to relent. His gods were no match for this new and stronger Hebrew Power. He was not dealing with a mere spokesman for the slaves, Moses. A stronger had come. Their armor or the protection offered by their gods was not adequate for the pervasive power sweeping over Egypt. Their only alternative was to release the slaves.

It is to this narrative that Jesus refers. He is the new Moses, the one greater than Moses. He has come to be the new warlord of the earth itself, the greater than Pharaoh. [Remember, Pharaoh himself was a supposed deity; one with the sun-god.] And he has come to liberate the captives, to set the slaves free, to lead the sons of Adam in a slave revolt.

Stripping the Strong Man of Power

Every exorcism, every liberation of an individual from Satan's power is an attack on the entire system of darkness. *"If I drive out demons by the finger of God, then the kingdom of God has come to you."* Every salvation is a spiritual warfare event. Follow the argument of Jesus, *"When a strong man, fully armed, guards his own house, his possessions are safe. But when someone stronger attacks and overpowers him, he takes away the armor in which the man trusted and divides up the spoils"* (Luke 11:21-22).

The strong man, who is fully armed, is Satan. The house, at the *micro* level, is the human body of the one man who is demonized. But at the *macro* level, it is corporate humanity, *Adam's house,* that is in view here. Satan has laid claim to Adam's house. At one level, his coup is rebellious and illegitimate, the act of a revolutionary tyrant; and at another, by Adam's sin, he has a legal standing. He guards Adam's house like a slave master and claims it and all born to Adam, as his own. He assumes, wrongly, that he is secure here; that his kingdom and his hold on the planet will never be reversed. His seized possessions, involving people and places, substance and spirit, are safe.

The 'Stronger One' is Christ. Despite all the armor Satan can muster, he is still no match for *the stronger*. Jesus acts here, not primarily from his divine power as God, but as the human Jesus, virgin born, perfect and sinless, and therefore the only man qualified to be the new king of earth. He is Jesus, born of Mary, by the Spirit, God incarnate, and yet fully man – the only unfallen man in history against whom Lucifer has no claim. In him is no fault. He is Jesus, the head of a new race of redeemed men, the one man who is fully surrendered to God, filled with the Spirit, and perfectly obedient to the Father. Jesus does not defeat Satan by drawing on innate divine powers. He defeats Satan by his perfect obedience as a man, and in doing so, he proves the worth of the human race and saves it from doom (Hebrews 5:8).

The house that Satan, the strong man, is guarding and holding hostage is Adam's house. He believed, wrongly, that he could establish a counter-kingdom on the foundation of the house of Adam. Like a group of rebel thugs who have taken over a small defenseless nation and brought it into a dark night of terror, Satan and his comrades have laid siege to the earth. But they have now been overtaken by someone stronger who has come to overpower, to reclaim people and possessions that are legally his, that he created and now comes to redeem.

It is clear that Jesus is no longer talking about the individual from whom has cast out a demon. He is talking about a much larger picture! He is talking about Satan's kingdom and Adam's house, drawing an analogy from the one demon, an agent of enslavement in collaboration with Satan, and the one demonized man under siege, to the larger concern of humanity's enslavement.

The Church – Agents of Liberation

The purpose of the sons of God, the bride of Christ, is to continue this liberation. In the name of Jesus (Phil. 2:10; John 16:24), we displace the denomic and release captives. Jude says of converts, we *"pull them from the fire...hating the garment spotted with the flesh"* (Jude 23). It is as if the judgment on the house of Adam has already begun, the structure is on fire. No one inside is safe. We are rescue agents, running inside the fiery structure to bring out the captive sons of Adam and make of them sons of God, by adoption.

Satan and his rebel angel band are united in one thing – their war against God and His Christ, by their exploitation of mankind. They are attempting to hold the planet hostage. They have Adam's sons and daughters, Adam's house under siege. We are the undercover operatives of the Kingdom that has come. It is here. It is now. And yet, it has not yet fully come. When Jesus returns, not only as priest and prophet, but as King; not only as Lamb, but as the Lion of the tribe of Judah (Revelation 5:5-6); as the servant-son (Hebrews 3:6), now revealed as the last in the line of King David (Isaiah. 16:5; Luke 1:32), to reclaim for eternity, his throne – the Kingdom will have fully come (Revelation 1:7; 19:11). And Satan will be bound (Revelation 20:2). And Christ will reign (Revelation 11:15; 20:6).

Until then, there are two streams of humanity in Adam's house. There are the sons of Adam, unredeemed, unwittingly cooperating with the illegal siege, to their own peril. And there are the sons of the revolution, who know that in the coming of Christ, something happened in the earth. And now we are charged with getting out the message. We are charged with proclaiming good news to the poor and disadvantaged, the poor in spirit. We are charged with healing broken hearts. We are charged with opening the prison to the captives. We are charged with opening the eyes to the blind and we might add, the ears of the deaf, the lips of the mute. We are charged with removing the shackles of the bound (Isaiah. 61:1f). We are liberators of those in Adam's house. We are in the uncomfortable, critical, strategic, bloody middle.

We have no idea, the place to which we have been exalted. It is a position higher than Adam every held. Because of the ministry of Jesus, and our relationship with him "... redeemed humanity outranks all other orders of created beings in the universe. Angels are created, not generated. Redeemed humanity is both created and generated, begotten of God, bearing His 'genes,' His heredity."[16]

> The Church...is already legally on the throne. Through the use of her weapons of prayer and faith she holds in this present throbbing moment the balance of power in world affairs. In spite of all of her lamentable weaknesses, appalling failures, and indefensible shortcomings, the Church is the mightiest force for civilization and enlightened social consciousness in the world today. The only force that is contesting Satan's total rule in human affairs is the Church of the Living God.[17]

We want prayer to be a quick prophetic declaration – a shout at the enemy who obediently cowers. It is more like a military campaign in guerilla warfare fashion. There is no clear line of attack. Uncertainty and unsettling upsurges come from unexpected quarters. And they come in bunches. While we might prefer a boxing match with the Evil One and the possibility of a supernatural knockout punch, the encounter is less like boxing and more like "wrestling" with dark powers.

Jesus waged warfare at the *macro* level. We wage warfare, one soul at a time, at the *micro* level. And as we do, we declare the coming of the acceptable year of the Lord, the year of Jubilee. That year was to be celebrated every fifty years, after a series of Sabbath years had been celebrated, once every seven years (Seven Sabbath

Years, once every seven years, equals 49 years. The next year, the 50th, was the Year of Jubilee.) Sadly, the Year of Jubilee was never celebrated, not once. And the Sabbath years were also ignored (2 Chronicles 36:20-21; Jeremiah 25:11). In the Year of Jubilee, social restitution took place. Debts were cancelled, so people could begin anew. In that year, the oppressed went free. The prisoners were set free. In that year, land grants and long-term losses were reversed. In that year, the rich gave to the poor, the advantaged helped the disadvantaged with a new start. Sadly, the church does not understand Jubilee. It has not accepted its role of being a liberating community. When Jesus returns, he will declare the kingdoms of this world his own and it will be a year of Jubilee (Leviticus 25:13f; 27:24f). He is looking for a Jubilee people now.

He has come to draw a line. *"He who is not with Me is against me, and he who does not gather with Me, scatters,"* Luke 11:23; Matthew 12:30. There are only two choices – with him, or against him. There is no neutral. This is a season of warfare for the planet. The word *gathers* here means *gathers to* or *with*. It is idea of being drawn to, the idea of unity. It implies a growing movement gathering around Christ as the liberator. He came to build 'his house,' his Church – the *ecclesia*, which means "called out" (Matthew 16:18). This growing movement of those called out of the crumbling house of Adam find in Christ, in the Church, a new house of refuge. It will not succumb to Satan. The gates of hell will not prevail against it. These are not the gates of the Church. They are "hell's gates." That is, they are the gates of Satan's illegal kingdom built on the foundation of the fallen house of Adam. Those who do not gather to Christ are part of a fragmented and doomed movement. Its feet are iron mixed with clay. Such elements do not bond (Daniel 2:42-43).

Lucifer – The Wounded Loser

> *When an evil spirit comes out of a man, it goes through arid places seeking rest and does not find it. Then it says, 'I will return to the house I left.' When it arrives, it finds the house swept clean and put in order. Then it goes and takes seven other spirits more wicked than itself, and they go in and live there. And the final condition of that man is worse than the first* (Luke 11:24-26).

Now, we are back to the *micro* – the individual. In bondage, muted by the demonic hold on him, the demonized man had no choice. Once liberated, the man has a choice. The demonic spirit that once possessed him is now displaced and disembodied. The dark power over him is broken. But that does not mean that the spirit will consider the exorcism final. And in this fact, we have our greater dilemma. Satan and his comrades appear more committed to defy Calvary and the Resurrection, than we are as the sons of light to enforce the victory of Christ's exaltation and enthronement in the heavens. Lucifer is relentless. We fight and win a small battle and consider the war over. We fail to post sentries. We assume that Lucifer and his imps are gracious losers. However, they are not. They will steal the trophy of your triumph right off your shelf - and that, due to a simple lack of persistence on our part.

The demon, displaced, now returns. Just as Satan, after the thousand year reign, will return and seek to deceive again. He refuses to accept defeat. He is unrepentant. He is incorrigible. After a one-thousand year prison sentence, he will return to his criminal life. The demon, too, displaced from the body of the man, has been searching for a clay temple from which he can operate, a human-being that will give him visibility, a puppet that he can bring under his power, but he has found none. That is only momentarily good news. Like a thief that has found a certain lock that is often unsecured, he comes back to strike again in the same location. Like a tramp that has trespassed and gained entry before, he will see if the house is available to him again. Surprisingly, he finds the man free, but unfortified. He finds the house empty, and not yet garnished. The liberated man, now set free, never fortified his residence. He never put locks on his door. He attempted to stay neutral. He did not use his freedom to secure his liberated state. Emptied of the awful foul spirit, he did not practice a holy communion with God that invited the Holy Spirit to occupy his clay temple. His only true choice of survival in this world system, on a planet with invisible rogue spirits, lay, in having the doorpost of his heart marked with the blood of the lamb. He must have thought that he could stand alone against the dark warring prince. But the powers were greater than himself. Matthew Henry says, "The heart of every unconverted sinner is the devil's palace, where he dwells, and where he rules."[18]

When a person is genuinely converted, there is the effect of "Christ's victory over the devil and his power in that soul, restoring the soul to its liberty, and recovering his own interest in it and power over it. All the endowments of mind or body are now employed for Christ."[19] That is not what happens in this passage. Something is amiss here. Matthew Henry believed,

> The house is swept from common sins, by a forced confession, as Pharaoh's; by a feigned contrition, as Ahab's; or by a partial reformation, as Herod's. The house is swept, but it is not washed; the heart is not made holy. Sweeping takes off only the loose dirt, while the sin that besets the sinner, the beloved sin, is untouched. The house is garnished with common gifts and graces. It is not furnished with any true grace; it is all paint and varnish, not real nor lasting. It was never given up to Christ, nor dwelt in by the Spirit...The wicked spirits enter in without any difficulty...welcomed...they dwell there; there they work, there they rule.[20]

The demon still advances a claim on the house – *"I will return to my house"* (Luke 11:24). We are never safe until we have delivered our souls fully to the Lordship of Jesus Christ.

So many Christians are free *from*, but not free *to* (1 Peter 2:26). They are not under the direct power of some demonic spirit, but neither are they fully under the influence of the Holy Spirit. They live in a supposed neutral zone (Romans 6:16). They are vulnerable in ways that they cannot understand.

The Binding of the Strong Man

Jesus came into Adam's house to bind the strong man, Satan. We often seek a 'macro' key for such binding. The key to power over the strongman is 'micro.' It is one soul at a time. It is the power of one (Romans 5:14-20). One man, Adam, succumbed to sin's control and Satan's manipulative and deceptive dominion. One man, Jesus, did not. And Satan left him (Matthew 4:11; Luke 4:13) – defeated. His temptations had no power over the last Adam. His deceptive ploys and power plays did not succeed. In this sense, Satan was bound, limited, his tactics were powerless with regard to Jesus. Lucifer will be bound (Revelation 20:2) in a macro sense, but that is an eschatological matter. Notice, nowhere in this passage does Jesus 'bind' the strong man or demon before the exorcism. In no instance does he practice 'macro' binding. Intercessors attempt to collectively bind the powers in their city – but for such a practice there is no biblical precedent.

Standing in the cross-hairs of the kingdom of darkness and the kingdom of light is the individual – and the battle is won or lost, one soul at a time. The nexus of control is in the power of the one - the one individual, the one heart. Who controls your life? By what spiritual power are you influenced? Have you invited Christ into your heart? Have you made him Lord? Are you under his discipline?

As individuals are won over, from darkness to light, from the body of Adam to the body of Christ, the victory of Christ in the earth is moved forward and Satan is defeated. We are called to the middle of this battleground.

Standing in the crowd is a perceptive woman. *"A certain woman of the company lifted up her voice, and said unto him, Blessed is the womb that bare thee ..."* (Luke 11:27). Perhaps the acclamation is innocent, perhaps it hints at the goddess cult, though doubtful, since it does not draw a sharp rebuke. And yet, it does generate a corrective note that makes the record of scripture. The triumph does not have its roots in Mary's conception or nurture, but in the power of obedience. It was by the disobedience of the one - Adam, and the ultimate obedience of the one – Jesus, that both subjugation and liberation comes. His comments are not meant to offer disrespect for his mother! She too had learned the power of obeying him. To the servants at the wedding feast she advised, *"Whatever He says, do it!"* (John 2:5) Jesus corrects the woman, *"Yea rather, blessed are they that hear the word of God, and keep it"* or obey it.

The chapter began with Jesus and his disciples in prayer together. And then he offered them a model, a template for prayer. He proceeded to tell a story that illustrated the most profound power of prayer, the power of the middle, the role of the intercessor. He offered an explanation on the implications of the story, he expanded their understanding of the principles in the story. And then Jesus gave us a graduate course on the middle.

The first man needed bread – salvation! And he was obviously hungry and ready to receive. The second man needed more than bread - he needed deliverance. He could not express his need or hear an offer for bread. Only liberation could bring him to a place of felt need. He was like the seed that the birds (demons) took away before it had time to germinate. Here too, someone must stand in the middle - defying Satan's kingdom and the authority of one of his demonic agents, while offering liberation to a son of Adam. The liberation of the house happens one soul at a time.

In World War I, the American troops and the Germans were yards away from one another in trench warfare. Neither side seemed willing to take the risk that would break the stalemate. The snowy winter countryside was blackened by shelling. The nights were cold and cruel. A German soldier, perhaps in a valiant attempt to break the standoff, ran through no-man's land toward the Allied trenches. He was immediately shot, he fell and was hopelessly entangled in barbed-wire. In the night, his cries for help were unsettling to both sides. Finally, an American soldier could no longer stand the sound of the tortured screams. He climbed out of the burrow and slid on his belly into and across no-one's land. With bullets flying inches over his head, he navigated his way under and through the barbed-wire. When his comrades realized what he was doing, they ceased fire. Then, when the Germans too understood his intent, they too ceased firing.

He reached the German soldier. He cut him free and stood him up - in the middle of no-one's land. Then he carried him, not back to the Allied Trenches as a prisoner of war, but straight into the German bunker. All guns in that section of the trench network were silent. Reaching the German lines, he delivered the wounded enemy. And then, placing him into the arms of his own brothers, he turned to return to his own side, as if that were permissible in war. A strong hand gripped his shoulder and spun him around. He stood face-to-face with a stern German officer in dead silence. Suspense filled the air. Then the German officer reached for the Iron Cross pinned to his own uniform, ripped it off, and pinned it on the American soldier, and gestured for him to return to his own company.

When he had safely reached his own trench, the volley of bullets continued. And the madness of war began again. This is the call of the believer. We venture into the uncomfortable middle, the bloody middle, hearing the cries of the wounded, and we somehow play a role in their liberation.

1. Tolkien, *The Lord of the Rings: The Return of the King*, 44.
2. Ibid, 46.
3. Ibid, 53-54.
4. Chuck Morse, *The Nazi Connection to Islamic Terrorism: Adolf Hitler and Haj Amin al-Husseini* (iUniverse Incorporated: Lincoln, NE, 2003), 78.
5. Chris Tiegreen, *Violent Prayer* (Multnomah: Sisters, Oregon; 2006), 75.
6. Ibid, 76.
7. Tolkien, *The Lord of the Rings: The Two Towers*, 118.
8. M. A. Haralson and John R. Hassell (1995). *Extracellular Matrix: A Practical Approach*. Ithaca, N.Y: IRL Press. ISBN 0-19-963220-0.
9. See the series, *"Shadow Over the Land"* and the tape: *Five Things That Defile the Land!* P. Douglas Small, produced by Alive Ministries.
10. Tolkien, *The Lord of the Rings: The Fellowship of the Ring*, 55
11. Ibid.
12. Ibid, 73.
13. Confer with Billheimer, 73.
14. Tolkien, *The Lord of the Rings: The Return of the King*.
15. The characteristic way this spirit or demon applied oppression to an individual was to mute them, to take away their capacity for speaking or hearing sound, to lock them into a world of silence. The idea is not that the demon was mute, but that the impact of his hold on the human was to silence that human.
16. Paul Billheimer, *Destined for the Throne* (Christian Literature Crusade: Fort Washington, PA; 1975), 15.
17. Ibid.
18. See *Matthew Henry Commentary*, notes on Luke 11:24: biblecommenter.com/luke/11-24.htm.
19. Ibid.
20. Ibid.

Discussion Guide

1. Discuss the idea of man as a temple of the Holy Spirit – a duplex with room for self, and yet room for God inside each human.

2. Talk about the fall of man and the result – man's identity with creation rather than the Creator.

3. Jesus came to re-secure the abandoned middle. The church is his partner in the middle on the earth-side, partnering with him, through Spirit-empowerment, to complete his mission. Agree or disagree?

4. Have you ever heard the concept of the two corporate men? Who are they? Born in Adam, we must die. True or false? How do we get from the dying Adam, into the living Christ?

5. Discuss the narrative of the exorcism. Can you separate the two conceptual pictures – the individual in need of deliverance and the house of Adam in need of liberation?

6. There are two other ways the concept is introduced – the house is Adam's house or family. The conflict of kingdoms is between the kingdom of God and the kingdom of darkness. Discuss this.

7. The Church is called to be an agent of liberation. Agree or disagree?

8. The house is liberated, then vacated, then in bondage again – How? Why?

9. We win the war one soul at a time. Agree or disagree?

10. What is the most important principle learned in this chapter?

ARAGON: *"The living have never used that road, for it is closed to them."*

THEODEN: *"Folk say that Dead Men out of the Dark Years guard the way and will suffer no living man to come to their hidden halls…the Dead come seldom forth and only at times of great unquiet and coming death."*

EOWYN: *"Yet it is said in Harrowdale, that in the moonless nights but a little while ago a great host in strange array passed by. Whence they came none knew, but they went up the stony road and vanished…"*[1]

CHAPTER TEN
STORIES FROM THE MIDDLE

Ruth Stull, and her missionary husband, ministered many years in Peru, in the Amazon basin. Receiving a call about a sick woman needing care, Ruth and two comrades went upstream a few hours in search of the needy woman to offer care. Rain in the Andes combined with melting snow had swollen the river. Ruth advised her friends that they should make haste and get back to their camp. The river's condition would only worsen. It did.

Downstream, they encountered a fallen tree. The swift current threw the boat against the tree with such force that Ruth was hurled out of the boat across the trunk of the tree. The swirling water created an undertow and she was hopelessly pulled to the bottom and entangled in vines. She fought to free herself in vain. She lost consciousness. And then, suddenly, she was above the surface of the water as if pushed up by some force, freed from the entangling vines. Those in the boat pulled her back on-board and then they continued downstream to camp.

As they arrived, Ruth found her husband prayerfully pacing, awaiting their arrival. He reported being griped with a tremendous burden, not for the sick woman to whom they had gone to minister, but for Ruth, as if he knew she faced some danger. This is the peculiar nature of the middle. It is mysterious. It is vague and at times defiant of a precise definition, and yet, simultaneously as real as mass and substance. And this is the critical place of intercession.

Weeks later, the Stull's would receive mail from supporters in America. Included were questions about their activities, and specifically, reports about mysterious prayer burdens. At a prayer meeting, one woman had enquired, "Has anyone heard any news about our missionaries, the Stull's?"

"It is strange that you would ask," another woman replied. "I was washing clothes and felt an urge to stop and immediately pray for them." Another woman reported, "I was washing dishes, and felt the same compelling urge." In all, twelve women had been independently summoned by the Spirit to the protective middle, all in the two week period leading up to the incident, and none afterward.

Sometimes, by the mystery of prayer, we man some invisible sentry post in the spirit-realm, watching out over some soul. Serving our time on the wall, with no con-

> *By the mystery of prayer, we man some invisible sentry post in the spirit-realm, watching out over some soul. Serving our time on the wall, with no contact with another watchman, we have no idea that we are small link in an otherwise undetected chain that has created a protective boundary...*

tact with another watchman, we have no idea that we are small link in an otherwise undetected chain that has created a protective boundary, a defensive circle. Distance and physical location matter little in such matters. The huddle of prayer somehow shields another from some danger. It affects outcomes. It changes real events. It stays the hand of the Evil One. Some rivers rage naturally, some spiritually. Jesus did not rebuke the wind and waves, he only needed to command them. A rebuke is not aimed at something neutral, but something spiritual. His rebuke was due to the spiritual nature of the storm.

The middle may at times provide a protective shield for a missionary. It may spare the life of some relative. It may peel back dark powers intent on destruction. It may be like the stand taken by Gandaff on the bridge, a declaration to dark dragon, "You will not pass!"[2]

Standing in the middle may invoke a protective intervention that forbids a deadly and untimely tragedy. Who can understand such things? The middle is such a powerful position.

The Middle – the Difference between Life and Death, Heaven and Hell

When Dr. Charles Blanchard was President of Wheaton College, he told a story about the power of persevering intercession. A man had become ill. His weight was less than 100 pounds. The doctors providing care were baffled by his illness. Standing by his bed, the attending physician announced his death to his wife. She was a Christian. Her husband was not.

"I'm sorry, we've lost him!" the attending physical reported.

"What do you mean that you have 'lost him?'" the Christian wife asked.

"He's dead," the physician reported, "there is nothing more we can do for him!"

"He can't be dead," she objected. "You see, I am a Christian.

And God promised me that he, too, would be a Christian – so he can't be dead. And even if he were dead, God would raise him from the dead so he could be saved."

Such a position is regarded, even by Spirit-filled Christians, as incredulous and presumptuous. There is such a thing as presumptuous faith. No one can force the hand of God. He alone is Sovereign. Claiming promises and demanding their execution and fulfillment by God is not Biblical. If it were, no one would die. No one would suffer. But that is not what is in view here. This woman had a promise from God - and that is different. It is intensely personal. No one can certify a God-given promise. Banks won't lend money on one. And weathermen won't change their forecast because of one. But, if you have been given such a promise, it is as good as gold. It is as certain to produce a storm as a cloud the size of a man's hand (1 Kings 18:44).

Abraham had a promise – and it came to pass (Genesis 18:10; 21:1-7). David was given a promise – and it came to pass (1 Samuel 16:12-13; 2 Samuel 2:1-4; 5:1-4). Prophets, speaking by the Spirit, saw their words come to pass and

> *The goal is never warfare or confrontation with dark powers. The goal is the reconciliation of lost people to God. That goal is possible only when the veil of blindness is lifted from hearts and minds, and that happens by persistent prayer in the contested, sometimes bloody, middle.*

true prophets still do. This woman believed because she had a promise from God. She demanded that another physician certify her husband's death. A second physician came. "He's dead," she was told. It wasn't enough.

Soon seven doctors were gathered around the lifeless body of her lost husband. She was now on her knees. "He can't be dead. He's not dead. And even if he were dead, God would raise him from the dead. He promised that he would be saved." One by one, the doctors slipped away. All assumed that she needed time to recover, time to accept the cold reality of her husband's death. She was left alone to grieve and come to her senses.

Some thirty minutes later, she called out for assistance. Was this the end of the siege? No, she needed a pillow. Her knees, she explained, were beginning to hurt.

An hour later, she was still by his bedside. Two hours. Three hours. Four hours. It was incredible. Unbelievable. Irrational. Insane. Five, then ten hours passed. Shifts changed at the hospital. Her reputation must have been growing. What was the hospital staff to do? Thirteen hours passed, as she quietly prayed by the bedside of her husband. Finally, he opened his eyes.

She calmly asked him, "What do you wish dear?"

"I want to go home," he replied.

"Then you shall," she promised. Suddenly doctors and nurses seemed to appear as if from thin air. They were checking vitals and ordering tests. They were astounded. They were in disbelief.

"If you take him home," they protested, "it will kill him."

"You told me that he was already dead," she countered. "I am taking him home."

And she did. That man recovered to become not only a

Christian, but a witness for Christ. A railroad engineer, he would testify of trips to various places to tell his story, a story of the power of persevering intercession.

If God gives you a word, for example, that a revival is coming, even if a church-doctor pronounces the congregation dead, believe God for a resurrection. Standing in the middle is not always easy. Experts may defy you. You may stand alone. Friends and family may abandon you. You may be belittled and ridiculed. Sincere faith partners may doubt. But your tenacity in the middle, your determination, and that only by the grace of God may be the difference between life and death for some soul you love, the city in which you live, the church at which you worship. You may have to "pull them out of the fire" (Jude 23) by determined prayer. Staying in the middle keeps mission stations and orphanages open. Staying in the middle opened the door to nations through the missionary efforts of men like David Livingston, William Cary and Adoniram Judson – and others.

The Middle – the Difference between Ministry Success and Failure

Dr. and Mrs. Jowett were assigned to a Mission – the Telegus Lone Star Mission of Ongole, India. But their work proved more difficult than anticipated. Finally, their supporting agency pulled the plug on the project. They would no longer fund it. They ordered the missionary and his family home. But time and tears had bonded the missionary couple to the dream. On the last morning, the day of the deadline, they climbed a hill overlooking the mission, with a 100-year-old Hindu convert named Julia. They greeted that dawn in prayer. They all prayed and they believed. They talked and then they prayed again. Julia later recounted, that it was unusual prayer – "they wrestled in prayer!" That morning, Dr. Jowett reported, as dawn came, he saw a great light, a supernatural light. The cactus field was suddenly transformed into a church with surrounding mission buildings – none of which were there. A sprawling mission compound lay before his eyes, one that existed only in the faith dimension. And yet, the scene was as real as anything tangible. He concluded that God was not finished.

> ARAGORN: Hold your ground, hold your ground! Sons of Gondor, of Rohan, my brothers! I see in your eyes the same fear that would take the heart of me. A day may come when the courage of men fails, when we forsake our friends and break all bonds of fellowship, but it is not this day. An hour of woes and shattered shields, when the age of men comes crashing down! But it is not this day! This day we fight! By all that you hold dear on this good Earth, I bid you, stand, Men of the West[13]

Almost immediately, the money came. And then the breakthrough came. Personnel came. After the prayer breakthrough, 2,222 were baptized in one day. In the course of that year, 10,000 came to faith in Christ. At one point, the compound grew to house the largest Christian church on the face of the earth. The hill on which the determining prayer was prayed, became known as "prayer meeting hill." It is legendary in missionary circles.[4]

That mission, one of the great and early successes in what would be identified later as the 10/40 window, came as a missionary couple stood 'in the middle,' by intercessory prayer, and saw from that vantage point a perspective only possible in spirit-led prayer. Standing in the middle, and deciding to stay the course, to see the vision come to pass, was the difference between success and failure.

The Middle and Nations

Sometimes, the battle for and in the middle, makes a difference for a nation! When Lester Sumrall was called to the Philippines, it was with the promise of a great revival. But the revival did not come. He preached – with virtually no results. The labor extended beyond weeks to months. He persisted. He refused to abandon the stubborn and unyielding middle. And yet, he became so involved in his own work that he was unaware of the frightful climate in the city created by young vixen, herself a victim.

All Clarita Villanueva had known was a life of tragedy. She had no recollection of her father. She could not recall if he had died or had simply deserted she and her mother. Her mother was a fortune-teller, a spiritualist. Clarita had been reared in a pagan environment, watching her mother conduct séances, communicate with the dead, and do clairvoyant readings for hire. With the money of her clients in her hand, she laughed as they left the house. It was a con-game to her, played with unsuspecting and gullible people.

Sadly, it was and is no game. Even the deceived are themselves often deceived. Before she was a teen, Clarita was left alone in the world. Her mother died. With no family to

> GALADRIEL: Your quest is known to us. I it was who first summoned the White Council. And if my designs had not gone amiss, it would have been governed by Gandalf the Grey...but even now there is hope left. I will not give you counsel, saying do this, or do that, nor in choosing this course or another. But this I will say to you: your Quest stands on the edge of a knife. Stray but a little and it will fail, to the ruin of all. Yet hope remains while all the Company is true. Do not let your heart be troubled. Go now and rest, for you are weary with sorrow and much toil.[5]

care for her, she was left to the streets. Only the prostitutes cared for her, teaching her their trade. At the age of 12, she was selling her body as a prostitute. She drifted from her island home to Manila, a center for money and vice. Again, the local harlots became her mentors and family. At the age of 17, she was picked up by the Manila police for soliciting.

She was placed in the ancient and notable Bilibid Prison. A prison for three centuries, the site was being used as the city jail. Two days after she was incarcerated, the most bizarre happening in the 300 year old history of the city occurred. Clarita was being bitten by unseen and unknown alien entities. Only she could see them – so the story goes. There were two of them, one larger than the other. The larger one, she described, was a huge monster-like spirit. Both had fangs that they sank deep into her flesh. She had bite marks on her back, her legs and arms. No human contortionist could have inflicted such wounds on himself. The marks were not human. And there was another mystery. The bite marks would appear simultaneously, and the blood that flowed from the wounds was mostly under her skin. She would scream in horror and faint.

The loud commotion echoed though the prison. Guards alerted medics, who came running to the women's division of Bilibid. There, Clarita was found twisting and turning, in a tormented state. She was taken to the prison hospital for observation, by a team of doctors. The medical team acknowledged that they had never encountered anything like they were witnessing.

The bizarre bite marks continued to appear, even in the prison hospital ward. It baffled all experts. University professors and medical experts were all invited to review the case. Appeals were sent to Filipino, Chinese and American physicians. The media picked up the story. Some ridiculed it. The story circled the globe. It was reported in Switzerland, France, Germany, England,

Canada, the United States – everywhere the strange phenomenon was front-page news at the time.

Some thought she was a witch, channeling dark energy. One doctor accused her of putting on an act. Clarita gazed at the doctor with snake-like eyes and said, "You will die." The doctor died the next day without any indication of sickness. Fear raced across the city - Clarita, it appeared, had the power to speak death. The chief jailer had also had confrontation with the rebellious Clarita. She cursed him and predicted his death. He was dead within four days. The whole prison seemed hostage to Clarita. Fear surrounded her. Authorities were paralyzed. No one knew how to help. Doctors called upon anyone and everyone for help. Three-thousand cables poured in from around the world offering advice, mostly from Japan and India, not one from a Christian nation. The only people to come to the prison to offer assistance were spiritualist, some of whom who suggested that it was John the Baptist who was biting her. The authorities asked them to leave.

For three awful weeks, this torture went on. Finally, a radio reporter came to Bilibid and audio taped a session in which doctors were violently struggling with Clarita, this demonized harlot. The reporter released his story on a local radio station, just after the 10 o'clock news. That night, in 1953, Lester Sumrall heard the radio report about Clarita Villanueva[6] He knew immediately what she was dealing with. All night he prayed and wept before the Lord, interceding for the city, for the girl, and for himself. Sumrall recalls, "I was living in a city that had a great need and I was not helping to meet that need. I was so busy putting up our church building and doing my own thing that I was not involved in the tragedy of Bilibid."

After a night of prayer, the Pentecostal preacher asked the mayor for permission to see Clarita. Authorities were reluctant to allow him, an American preacher, access, fearing consequences. Sumrall listened to their warnings and agreed to take full responsibility for the consequences of his visit. They had no faith in his ability to solve the problem or offer insights. After all, he was not a trained psychologist. He was a mere preacher without impressive credentials. He arrived at the prison as the funeral cortege for the chief jailer was leaving. He recalls, "I have never seen such a fearful and perplexed group of people as those I met in that prison that day. They were afraid that this thing would kill them as it had the two others who dared cross it. It was their responsibility to do something for the girl, yet they had no earthly idea what to do about the situation."

At the prison, the authorities were sceptical and resistant to his seeing Clarita. Sumrall was asked to wait. A large group of news reporters, foreign members of the press, university professors and medical doctors had been invited by Dr. Lara, the head physician of the prison, to consult on the matter of Clarita. As she was led into the meeting room, she passed reporters, professors and doctors without incident. They were important. Sumrall was a nobody. But when Clarita saw Sumrall, a dramatic showdown followed. She screamed at him violently. She spoke perfect English to him, knowing none. She cursed him. She cursed Jesus and the blood of Jesus. Sumrall said that he entered into the battle of his life. What followed was not an exorcism, but serial exorcisms. Sumrall looked at the young girl and past her at the same time. "I know you hate me. I have come to cast you out," speaking not to Clarita but to the Evil Spirit who had taken her hostage. That was the beginning of the confrontation. A raging battle followed with the girl blaspheming God – the Father, God – the Son, and God – the Holy Spirit. Her eyes burned like coals of fire full of hate. Sumrall commanded the evil spirit to loose her. After a three-day confrontation, she relaxed, smiled, and said, "He's gone."

Sumrall recalled asking Clarita, "Which way did he go!" With a straight face, she pointed, "He went that way!" Dr. Lara, the prison physician took Sumrall to the Mayor's office to announce the victory, "Mayor, the devil is dead!" Newspapers reported, "The Devil loses round one!" Sumrall told the Mayor, the girl is healed. Indeed, she was.[7]

Paul, in Ephesus, had confronted the slave girl whose sinister bond with dark powers affected the whole city. And her deliverance brought a breakthrough. The Evil One understands the power of the middle more than we do. Jesus serves as the intercessor, in the upper middle position, in and from heaven itself. And we, his bride-partner, operate as intercessors with him on earth. He is in heaven, in the 'upper-middle.' We are on the earth, in the 'lower middle' – agreeing with him in prayer for the kingdom of God to break into the time-space world. Satan, the prince and power of the air, seeks to replicate this process. He operates out of the middle heaven looking for ground contacts through whom he can discharge his wicked energy and accomplish his ominous purposes. The middle is a crowded and contested place.

There are times, when only the neutralizing of these intermediary powers can change the climate of a city or nation and open it to the kind of powerful advances God desires for his kingdom. We do not nor should we seek such encounters. We back into them. We do not hunt for the demonic, nor are we pursuers of dark knowledge. Such practices are seductive. The darkness finds us. And when it stands before us, when it defies us, when it entrenches itself, when it is an evident fountain of death wielding wicked influence, we have no choice but to confront the powers and pray that the Evil One's hold be broken. When such an effective disconnect takes place, it prevents a noxious anesthesia from pouring into the city and bringing even the godly under its spell. We do not engage such powers in order that God might move. Victories come because God is moving.

The deliverance of Clarita led to a huge Christian revival in the Philippines.

When Clarita was free, the Philippines, at least certain people in Manila were freed. The result was 150,000 conversions that took place almost immediately. Many point to that incident as the turning point for the Philippines. It opened the heavens over the nation.

Standing in the middle is standing in a contested place. Lucifer has claimed it. In the face of the Resurrection, the Ascension and the Enthronement of Jesus, Satan persists in his madness and continues to masquerade as the king of the earth. Christ, by his own blood, has fought a battle to re-secure the middle. His resurrection affirms his indestructibility. Still, Satan continues to contest the middle. He refuses to surrender the ground. There are times when a breakthrough will require head-to-head confrontation with evil powers.

The goal is never warfare or confrontation with dark powers. The goal is the reconciliation of lost people to God. That goal is possible only when the veil of blindness is lifted from hearts and minds, and that happens by persistent prayer in the contested, sometimes bloody, middle.

The Strategic Middle – the Launching Ground for Ministries

Sometimes, the power of the middle is as far-reaching as the story of Clarita, even if it is not as dramatic. Dorothy Clapp was a suburban housewife who lived next door to a New Jersey high school. Acts 17:26 says that God orders our boundaries. Dorothy felt challenged to pray for her neighbor, the school. She did so quietly and consistently for a decade. Then God redirected her focus. He moved her to begin to pray specifically for students and their conversion. After some time, she heard about George Verwer. George was a natural leader. The problem was that he was not setting a good example, but a bad one.

Dorothy sent him a Gospel of John, some Christian literature, and informed him that she was praying for him. After more persistent prayer, George came to faith in Christ. When he did, his influence was so far reaching, that almost 300 kids in the high school came to faith as well. In Christmas of 1957, he went to Mexico with two other students in a beaten up old truck, loaded with Spanish Gospel literature. The next summer, they took another mission trip, and then another. Each year, the number of teams grew. Each year, they touched more places on the face of the earth than the year before. Today, 5400 people are involved in that now global movement – Operation Mobilization (OM). The ministry serves 110 countries.

Sometimes standing in the middle can set off a chain of events that launches a global movement. One woman - and one teenage conversion. One young man, prayed into the kingdom, and now as a result, thousands of young men and women yearly engage in Christian ministry. The small closet in which Dorothy Clapp prayed is now much larger. Her tiny space in the middle has been enlarged.[8]

The Critical Middle – and the Climate of a City

Ed Silvoso often shares the story of his hometown of San Nicolas, Argentina. Near the end of the last century, cult worship related to the Queen of Heaven took over the city. No one noticed the connection and none probably dared to assert one. But soon, industries had shut down. Commerce came to a standstill. Crime increased. The police were no match for a growing criminal element. The anemic church experienced ugly splits. Pastors died too young. The spiritual climate of the city was toxic and repressive.

Then, in the summer of 1996, almost 400 prayer delegates from four continents converged on the city and joined locals in prayer. They prayed at the gates of the city. They held services in churches throughout the city, repenting of sin in the church and in the city. The purpose was cleansing, and laying responsibility for the condition of the city, on the back of the church. Silvoso says, "Every major problem in the city (macrocosm) is always a magnified expression of unresolved problems in the Church (microcosm). Darkness can only prosper in the absence of light."[9]

Following a day of repentance, pastors at the gates of the city, drove stakes into the ground and made prophetic declarations over the city. They declared the city, a place of victory and not of defeat. They proclaimed, "Jesus is the Lord of the city, not the Queen of Heaven." They declared that the blood of Christ, was shed for the city and its people. Jesus had paid for the city – and for a revival in its streets. The proclamation was broadcast on radio stations and went throughout the city. Unity services were held all over the city with a strategy of demonstrating denominational diversity in unity.

Believers were then challenged to dedicate their homes as mission stations for the neighborhood. They were challenged to cleanse their homes. And then, to prayer-walk their neighborhoods. All over the city, on the same day, Christians were out on the streets, in areas where they lived, praying for their neighbors. The entire city was touched and prayed over in a day.

The crime rate, which had been out of control, dropped dramatically. During the next week, following that prayer, not one crime was reported. Pastors repented for division. Public officials asked for prayer from city pastors. Prodigals returned to Christ. In that week, the church had intentionally stepped into the middle, into the role of intercession. It had functioned as a prophetic voice, declaring into the spirit-realm, and into heaven, their desire for Jesus to be Lord. They invited him to come to the city. They functioned in a priestly role. They prayed for the reconciliation of the city to God, of churches one to another, of sinners to the Savior, for peace! And the peace of God settled over the whole city.[10]

This is the power of the intentional middle. The power of intercession.

---

1. Tolkien, *The Lord of the Rings: The Return of the King*, 63.
2. From a scene in *"The Lord of the Rings."*
3. Tolkien, *The Lord of the Rings: The Return of the King*.
4. Lester Sumrall, Alien Entities. *A Look Behind the Door to the Spirit Realm* (Whitaker House: PA, 1995), 131-138.
5. Charles Cowman, *Springs in the Valley* (Grand Rapids, MI; 1997), 218-219.
6. Tolkien, *The Lord of the Rings: The Two Towers*, 400-401.
7. Sumrall.
8. www.omcanada.org/about/history.php
9. Ed Silvoso, *Prayer Evangelism*, 28.
10. Ibid, 27-30.
11. Tolkien, *The Lord of the Rings: The Return of the King*, 290.

Discussion Guide

1. Have you ever had an experience similar to the intercessors who were prompted by the Spirit to pray for Ruth Stull?

2. The story told by Dr. Blanchard is so incredible. Do you think we might experience more such miracles if we stood more firmly on the ground of faith? Or do you fear that such a shift would only produce presumptuous embarrassments for the Kingdom of God?

3. What about the visionary experience of Dr. Jowett? Have you ever had such a moment, when you saw what could be, what might be, if you could persist in prayer and faith? What happened? What was the outcome?

4. The breakthrough that came did so on the cusp of abandonment of the mission. What if they had given up? Would the breakthrough have still come?

5. Clarita Villanueva was also 'in the middle' on the dark side, of course? How does that work? Is someone in your community on the dark side, channeling spiritual influence into your community?

6. At times we seem to glorify the dark powers, and at other times we ignore them. How do we find balance?

7. The story of Sumrall, a common and formally untrained preacher, in the middle of a sea of doctors and trained therapists - and God uses him to bring a cure to Clarita. Do you think we disqualify ourselves? Lack confidence? Could God give us some cure to some community problem for which we have no formal training – because the solution was not so much medical or scientific, as it was spiritual?

8. When Clarita was freed, the city seemed to be freed at the same time. When the slave girl was freed in Acts 16, Ephesus had a revival. Discuss such connections. What are their implications?

9. Dorothy Clapp adopted the school next door and then a specific student. The result was and is a global ministry. What and who could you adopt for prayer?

10. When Ed Silvoso began to pray for the city - the crime rate fell. God intervened. The city was impacted. Can you believe that God would do that for your city?

Galadriel: With water from the stream Galadriel filled the basin to brim and breathed on it, and when the water was still again she spoke. *"I have brought you here so that you may look in it, if you will."*

The air was very still, and the dell was dark.

Frodo: *"What shall we see?"*

Galadriel: *"The mirror will show things unbidden, and those are often stranger and more profitable than things which we wish to behold. What you will see, I cannot tell. The mirror shows things that were, and things that are, and things that yet may be. Even the wisest cannot always tell. Do you wish to look?"*

Frodo peered into the liquid mirror. Scenes of the future danced before him powerfully, exposing the ring of power. They were dismal scenes, and the strength of the darkness was so forceful that he was thrown backward to the ground, his face grimacing with pain and anxiety as the uncertain peril.

Galadriel: *"I know what you saw. It is what will come to pass if you should fail."*

Gandalf: *"Are you in pain, Frodo?"*

Frodo: *"Well, yes I am. It is my shoulder. The wound aches, and the memory of darkness is heavy on me. "*

Gandalf: *"Alas, there are some wounds that cannot be wholly cured."*

Frodo: *"I fear it may be so with mine. There is no real going back. Though I may come to the Shire, it will not seem the same; for I shall not be the same."* [11]

Alive Publications, an outreach of Alive Ministries: PROJECT PRAY, is an independent small publisher that specializes in prayer and prayer-evangelism resources for individuals, small groups and local churches. The ministry also produces resource kits, with companion videos and study guides that accompany several of their books.

PRAYER – THE HEART OF IT ALL
Discusses prayer fundamentals; the four critical elements: at-home daily prayer, the church at prayer, intercessory prayer and prayer evangelism; and how to apply each of these to create a great awakening in yourself, your church, your sphere influence and the world. Book $14.99; Personal and Group Study Guide $14.99; Resource Kit $99.99

THE PRAYER CLOSET
CREATING A PERSONAL PRAYER ROOM
What we seek is more than a place, more than mere words or even a disciplined, noble routine. It is more than the fact that we pray daily or the function of prayer and its benefits – it is relationship that, to be transforming, has be centered in the heart. Prayer is not something we do, it is someone we are with. And that needs a place! Book $16.95; Resource Kit $74.99

THE GREAT EXCHANGE - WHY YOUR PRAYER REQUESTS MAY NOT BE GETTING ANSWERS
The lack of answers to our prayers is not because God no longer answers or does not want to help. It is often an issue on our side – some hindrance to prayer, blockages in our own heart. Learn practical steps to answered prayer! Book $14.99; Personal and Group Study Guide $14.99; Resource Kit $129.99

ENTERTAINING GOD AND INFLUENCING CITIES Prayer is not about words and requests. It is not even the first and foremost about intercession. That will come. Prayer is about hosting God in a world from which He has been excluded. Book $14.99; CD $8; DVD $15

PRINCIPLES OF WORSHIP
A Study of the Tabernacle of Moses. Descriptions of the purpose of each piece as a template for prayer. A study that goes beyond review of details, this study is rich with spiritual insights.
Book $19.99; 4 CD Set $25; 2 DVD Set $25
Book with Powerpoint Resource $80

www.alivepublications.org

THE PRAYING CHURCH HANDBOOK

- A collection of substantive reflections on prayer.
- Contributors include global and national leaders, as well as Church of God authors, leaders and intercessors.

4 VOLUME SET

VOLUME I
Foundations
(664 pages)

VOLUME II
Personal and Family Prayer
(714 pages)

VOLUME III
The Pastor and the Congregation
(716 printed pages; 428 pages on disc)

VOLUME IV
Intercessory Prayer and Mission
(732 printed pages; 587 pages on disc)

WWW.ALIVEPUBLICATIONS.ORG

Schools of Prayer

Training focused on learning, experiencing and leading in the area of prayer. Schools of Prayer are facilitated by P. Douglas Small or through our new associate presenter program. Our glorious role is help people begin to recover a Biblical view of prayer, one that is not merely transactional and acquisitional, but also transformational.

The Prayer Closet: Creating a Personal Prayer Room
What we seek is more than mere words or a disciplined, noble routine for prayer. Prayer is a relationship that has to be centered in the heart. Prayer is not something we do, it is someone we are with. And that needs a place!

The Great Exchange: Why Your Prayer Requests May Not Be Getting Answers
Prayer works, because God works. It is effective, because its hope is in Him and His action. But it also demands changes in us. Learn practical steps to answered prayer!

PRAYER – The Heart of It All
Grow deeper in your prayer life by discovering why God wants us to pray. Discover how to: develop a personal prayer life; pray together as a family; start a prayer ministry in your church; prayer missionally for others and for a Great Awakening.

www.projectpray.org
1-855-84-ALIVE

PRAYING CHURCH MOVEMENT

JOIN THE MOVEMENT

A network of local prayer leaders who are on a journey to bring prayer to the heart of all they do.

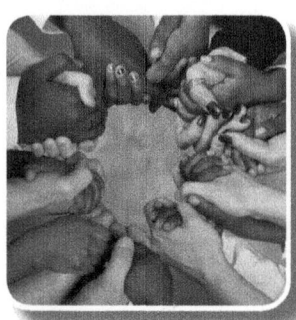

- Be encouraged
- Challenged
- Inspired and
- Resourced

REGISTER FOR FREE
OR BECOME A PREMIUM MEMBER FOR EVEN MORE VALUE!

WWW.PROJECTPRAY.ORG

AS PART OF THE MOVEMENT BECOME A

Certified Prayer Trainer

Join others who affirm the goals of the Praying Church Movement and facilitate groups of prayer leaders from various churches to create an on-going forum for learning, training and encouragement.

- Prayer Training
- Tool-time - Fresh Resources
- Talk-it-over/Take-it-home Application
- Quarterly Continuing Education